Praise for *What If Jesus Was Serious*?

When Jesus is listened to, really listened to, His words always come to life because they are living words. They have life and they give life. Skye has really listened to them and has responded with this life-giving book. Like Jesus' words, it is surprising and shocking and frustrating and alive in its own way.

MICHAEL CARD
Faith-based musician, author, and teacher

I found it hard to read more than 3–4 pages without stopping, as it forced me to strongly consider what God was saying to me, through this fresh look at Jesus' words in His most famous sermon. For many of us, the Sermon on the Mount has become too familiar for our own good. We've neutered it by this familiarity, and often miss the way it was designed to bring us to our knees. I'm going to be reading this for years to come. Skye remains a gift to the church, and a prophetic voice that we desperately need for these challenging times!

KEVIN PALAU
President of the Luis Palau Association

"What if Jesus Was Serious?" is a stellar step forward in Skye Jethani's mission to help us all consider the reality of God's kingdom and Jesus' outstanding invitation to us to live life with Him. Full of whimsy that only makes Skye's insights hit harder, this is a book I'd recommend to anyone who is tired of religious games and wants to truly consider who Jesus is and what He might be saying to us today.

MICHAEL WEAR
Author of *Reclaiming Hope: Lessons Learned in the Obama White House about the Future of Faith in America*

This book is exactly what I've been looking for: a deep dive into Jesus' most powerful teachings merged with Skye's provocative insights and application to life and culture today.

KARA POWELL
Executive Director of the Fuller Youth Institute and coauthor of *Growing Young* and *Growing With*

Skye Jethani always makes you think with his fresh but faithful approaches to Scripture. Too often we are tempted to be, as James warns us, hearers but not doers of the Word. Skye challenges us to not only listen to Jesus but to obey Him. His creative study here of the most famous sermon in history will challenge you, comfort you, and most importantly, provoke you to take Jesus seriously. I encourage you to use this resource with your church or small group.

DANIEL DARLING
VP of Communications for ERLC; author of several books, including *The Dignity Revolution* and *The Characters of Christmas*

What If Jesus Was Serious? is witty, incisive, and a fresh perspective on the teachings of Jesus. We too often stroll past the revolutionary call of Jesus to give up our possessions and follow Him. Skye Jethani helps us pause, look a bit deeper, and consider what Jesus actually meant in and through His teachings.

SCOTT HARRISON
New York Times bestselling author, *Thirst*

The content—and the style—of Skye's book are unique. But so is Skye. In his consistent and valuable manner, Skye helps us understand the age-old truths of Jesus' call to follow Him, but in new and fresh ways. Clear. Prophetic. Whimsical. Corrective. Insightful. As a visual learner, I loved this book. And I'm confident you will, too.

J. R. BRIGGS
Founder, Kairos Partnerships; author of *The Sacred Overlap* and *Fail*

Skye offers us a user-friendly guide to the bedrock teaching of Jesus. *What If Jesus Was Serious?* provides new depth of insight for those who are familiar with the Sermon on the Mount and accessible footholds for those who are new in their faith.

ROBERT GELINAS
Lead Pastor, Colorado Community Church, and author of *Discipled by Jesus: Your Ongoing Invitation to Follow Christ*

We have done everything in our relationship to Jesus over the years. We have taken Him personally, politically, culturally, religiously, but when it comes to discipleship, we have somehow evaded actually taking Jesus seriously. In this compelling and challenging book, Skye does a masterful job of casting a vision of what serious discipleship looks like. Highly recommended.

JON TYSON
Author of *Beautiful Resistance*; Lead Pastor, Church of the City New York

WHAT IF JESUS WAS SERIOUS?

A VISUAL GUIDE TO THE TEACHINGS OF JESUS WE LOVE TO IGNORE

SKYE JETHANI

MOODY PUBLISHERS

CHICAGO

Some content in this book was previously published on the author's blog or in email devotionals.

Unless otherwise indicated, all Scripture quotations are from the ESV® Bible (The Holy Bible, English Standard Version®), copyright © 2001 by Crossway, a publishing ministry of Good News Publishers. Used by permission. All rights reserved.

Scripture quotations marked (NIV) are taken from the Holy Bible, New International Version®, NIV®. Copyright © 1973, 1978, 1984, 2011 by Biblica, Inc.™ Used by permission of Zondervan. All rights reserved worldwide. www.zondervan.comThe "NIV" and "New International Version" are trademarks registered in the United States Patent and Trademark Office by Biblica, Inc.™

Edited by Kevin P. Emmert
Interior and cover design: Erik M. Peterson
Interior and cover illustrations: Skye Jethani

All websites and phone numbers listed herein are accurate at the time of publication but may change in the future or cease to exist. The listing of website references and resources does not imply publisher endorsement of the site's entire contents. Groups and organizations are listed for informational purposes, and listing does not imply publisher endorsement of their activities.

Library of Congress Cataloging-in-Publication Data

Names: Jethani, Skye, 1976- author.
Title: What if Jesus was serious? : a visual guide to the teachings of
   Jesus we love to ignore / Skye Jethani.
Description: Chicago : Moody Publishers, 2020. | Includes bibliographical
   references. | Summary: "Let's face it. A lot of Christian resources can
   feel cheesy, out-of-touch, and a little boring. But when Skye Jethani
   started doodling and writing up some of his thoughts about God, his
   Twitter and email list blew up. What If Jesus Was Serious? is a
   compilation of all-new reflections (and hand-drawn doodles) from Skye.
   He takes a look at some of Jesus' most demanding teachings in the Sermon
   on the Mount and pushes us to ask whether we're really hearing what
   Christ is saying. The visual component of the book makes it memorable
   and enjoyable to read, and Skye's incisive reflections make it
   worthwhile for any Christian. If you've traditionally been dissatisfied
   with Christian devotional resources but love to learn about Jesus and
   think deeply, this book was written for you"-- Provided by publisher.
Identifiers: LCCN 2019058733 (print) | LCCN 2019058734 (ebook) | ISBN
   9780802419750 (paperback) | ISBN 9780802498687 (ebook)
Subjects: LCSH: Sermon on the mount--Meditations. | Sermon on the
   mount--Illustrations. | Christianity--United States--21st century. |
   Christianity and culture--United States--History--21st century. | Jesus
   Christ--Example. | Christian life.
Classification: LCC BT380.3 .J48 2020 (print) | LCC BT380.3 (ebook) | DDC
   226.9/06--dc23
LC record available at https://lccn.loc.gov/2019058733
LC ebook record available at https://lccn.loc.gov/2019058734

Originally delivered by fleets of horse-drawn wagons, the affordable paperbacks from D. L. Moody's publishing house resourced the church and served everyday people. Now, after more than 125 years of publishing and ministry, Moody Publishers' mission remains the same—even if our delivery systems have changed a bit.

Moody Publishers
820 N. LaSalle Boulevard
Chicago, IL 60610

3 5 7 9 10 8 6 4

Printed in the United States of America

For Dave Schreier

"For whoever does the will of my Father in heaven
is my brother."

CONTENTS

	CHRISTIAN CULTURE	POST- CHRISTIAN CULTURE

KING

KINGDOM {

CHRISTIAN CULTURE	POST-CHRISTIAN CULTURE
HUMAN DIGNITY	HUMAN DIGNITY
JUSTICE	JUSTICE
EQUALITY	EQUALITY
MERCY	MERCY
PEACE	PEACE
PROGRESS	PROGRESS
FLOURISHING	FLOURISHING

Introduction

WHAT'S OUR PROBLEM?

FOLLOWING JESUS HAS never been easy, but some believe it's becoming even more difficult as Western cultures become increasingly post-Christian. Today, fewer people identify as "Christian," fewer attend church with any regularity, and the fastest growing religious group in the United States is the so-called Nones—those with no religious affiliation. Along with these demographic changes, fewer people see the Bible as a source for moral or spiritual wisdom, and popular attitudes toward traditional Christian sexual ethics now reside somewhere between indifference and hostility.

As a result, some Christians who once felt welcomed and accepted by the culture now feel pushed to the edges of the public square. It's natural to interpret this marginalization as a kind of cultural punishment, the natural outcome of holding on to beliefs and values the society would prefer to abandon. This has led some Christians to cry "Persecution!" and assume the posture of victims, and no doubt there are real cases of unjust hostility toward followers of Jesus. In response to this social banishment, these embattled believers sometimes assemble into political platoons to fight the culture war with the goal of retaking the land for Jesus.

This interpretation of the current cultural landscape assumes Christians are marginalized because we take Jesus too seriously. This view says if we'd just relax, hold our faith more loosely, and let popular values override biblical ones then we'd find more acceptance in the culture.

But what if we have it backwards? What if the underlying malady afflicting Christians today isn't that we take Jesus too seriously, but that we've failed to take Him seriously enough? What if much of the culture's judgment of Christians isn't the result of obeying Jesus, but the result of Christians ignoring Him?

Several years ago, I taught a class at my church on the Sermon on the Mount—Jesus' most famous message, which contains many of our faith's most important ethical teachings. On the first day of the class, after reading the full sermon together, I asked the students, "How many of you think Jesus actually expects us to live out these commands?" No one raised their hand. I was surprised, so I dug a deeper. I asked, "Why shouldn't we take the Sermon on the Mount seriously?"

"It's impossible to obey," one person said. "No one can live like this."

"Jesus was just showing how we all need God's grace," another student shared. "He was illustrating what a perfect life looks like and how none of us can attain it."

In their view, Jesus must have preached this sermon while frequently winking at His disciples to communicate, "Don't worry. You don't have to take any of this seriously." Never mind that He ended the sermon with a story about the perils of not obeying His words. Today, many Christians simply dismiss the

Sermon on the Mount as irrelevant, even as they stridently proclaim their allegiance to Jesus in the culture.

Consider an interview a Christian leader had with a reporter in 2018. The reporter asked why so many Christians were willing to support political candidates who revel in disobeying Jesus' teachings. "I think they are finally glad that there's somebody on the playground that is willing to punch the bully," the Christian leader replied.

"What happened to turning the other cheek?" the reporter asked, referring to Jesus' words in the Sermon on the Mount about nonretaliation.

"You know, you only have two cheeks," the Christian replied.[1]

Still, the Christian leader's point is revealing. He apparently thinks Jesus' words in the Sermon on the Mount are to be followed *up to a point*. Once important things are at risk, like political power, it's okay to ignore Jesus' commands. I call this the "Only Two Cheeks" excuse, and it's one I've heard a lot.

In my class on the Sermon on the Mount, one student offered a version of this excuse when he said, "Jesus' commands aren't practical. If we took Him seriously, people would walk all over us." Others agreed. Loving your enemies, turning the other cheek, and giving to anyone who asks is foolish. It's no way to get ahead, let alone survive, in a dangerous world.

"Was Jesus a fool for following these ideas Himself?" I asked. "After all, by loving His enemies He ended up on a Roman cross." I had the class in a corner. None of these good, Christian people wanted to call Jesus a fool, but they didn't want to say His teachings were important for us to follow, either.

This tension between praising Jesus and actually obeying

Him explains why so much of contemporary Christianity has lost its moral authority and spiritual credibility. On Sunday, contemporary Christians are eager to worship a crucified Savior who loved and forgave His enemies. But on Monday, we want permission to behave like the schoolyard bully who uses fear and anger to get ahead.

Once we recognize how eager contemporary Christians are to dismiss the Sermon on the Mount, our perception within the broader culture begins to make more sense. For example, data compiled by numerous researchers have found, "Evangelical Christians are as likely to embrace lifestyles every bit as hedonistic, materialistic, self-centered, and sexually immoral as the world in general."[2] And Christian researcher George Barna concluded, "American Christianity has largely failed since the middle of the twentieth century because Jesus' modern-day disciples do not act like Jesus."[3] All this confirms why the culture generally views Christians as hypocrites. Statistically speaking, we are.

Far from being hostile toward Jesus' message, my experience has been that our society is hungry for precisely the kind of integrity, gentleness, kindness, and love Jesus reveals in His sermon. We who claim to be Jesus' followers and seek a life shaped by His kingdom hold the antidote to the division and anger that is poisoning our culture. If we want the culture to take Jesus more seriously, maybe we should try it first. After that, if the culture still rejects Christians and our message, at least it will be for the right reason. That's what this book is all about. Let's begin . . .

PART 1

WHO IS REALLY BLESSED?

Seeing the crowds, he went up on the mountain, and when he sat down, his disciples came to him.

And he opened his mouth and taught them, saying:

"Blessed are the poor in spirit, for theirs is the kingdom of heaven.

"Blessed are those who mourn, for they shall be comforted.

"Blessed are the meek, for they shall inherit the earth.

"Blessed are those who hunger and thirst for righteousness, for they shall be satisfied.

"Blessed are the merciful, for they shall receive mercy.

"Blessed are the pure in heart, for they shall see God.

"Blessed are the peacemakers, for they shall be called sons of God.

"Blessed are those who are persecuted for righteousness' sake, for theirs is the kingdom of heaven.

"Blessed are you when others revile you and persecute you and utter all kinds of evil against you falsely on my account. Rejoice and be glad, for your reward is great in heaven, for so they persecuted the prophets who were before you."

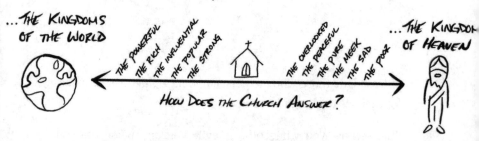

WHO IS REALLY BLESSED ACCORDING TO...

...THE KINGDOMS OF THE WORLD

...THE KINGDOM OF HEAVEN

THE POWERFUL · THE RICH · THE INFLUENTIAL · THE POPULAR · THE STRONG

THE OVERLOOKED · THE PEACEFUL · THE PURE · THE MEEK · THE SAD · THE POOR

HOW DOES THE CHURCH ANSWER?

1 IF JESUS WAS SERIOUS . . . THEN WE WILL FOCUS MORE ON HIS GOOD NEWS AND LESS ON RELIGIOUS TO-DO'S.

IT'S DANGEROUS WHEN religious people read the Bible. They are often tempted to make the particular into the universal. For example, in the Gospels, Jesus called Peter to leave his fishing business to become His apostle and a "fisher of men." Rather than seeing this as Peter's particular calling, those steeped in religion often insist this is a universal expectation upon all

Christians. While heaping on the guilt, they conveniently ignore other stories where Jesus gives would-be disciples callings very different from Peter's. Jesus even tells some who want to follow Him to "go home." The gospel writers did not tell the story of Peter's calling to prescribe what all believers should do. The story was simply meant to describe what Peter *did* do.

The same temptation to confuse *de*scription for *pre*scription is at play when we read the opening of the Sermon on the Mount. In the first twelve verses, known as the Beatitudes, Jesus identifies who is blessed by God. His list includes the poor in spirit, those who mourn, and the meek. Some misread this section as prescriptive—as what we should seek to be if we desire God's blessing. Such a reading will lead us to believe being joyful or courageous is ungodly, and that sadness and weakness are true signs of spiritual maturity. That, of course, is nonsense.

Jesus is not prescribing how to be blessed, but rather describing who is blessed. While the world says the strong, powerful, and happy are "well off," Jesus turns our expectations upside down by saying it's the weak, sad, and overlooked who are well off in God's kingdom. Stanley Hauerwas puts it this way:

> *Too often those characteristics [of the Beatitudes] . . .*
> *are turned into ideals we must strive to attain. As ideals,*
> *they can become formulas for power rather than descrip-*
> *tions of the kind of people characteristic of the new age*
> *brought by Christ. . . . Thus Jesus does not tell us that we*
> *should try to become poor in spirit, or meek, or peace-*
> *makers. He simply says that many who are called into*
> *the kingdom will find themselves so constituted.*[1]

The beginning of the Sermon on the Mount is not a to-do list; it is a good news list. Jesus is describing who has the most to gain by the arrival of His kingdom. He is not prescribing what you must do to enter it.

 READ MORE **1 Samuel 16:7; Luke 13:22–30**

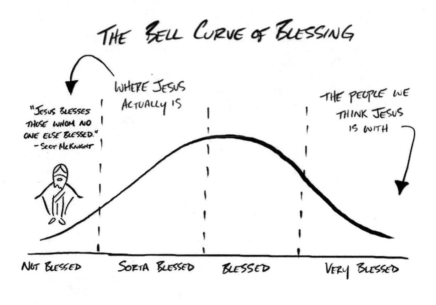

THE BELL CURVE OF BLESSING

"JESUS BLESSES THOSE WHOM NO ONE ELSE BLESSED."
— SCOT McKNIGHT

WHERE JESUS ACTUALLY IS

THE PEOPLE WE THINK JESUS IS WITH

NOT BLESSED SORTA BLESSED BLESSED VERY BLESSED

2 IF JESUS WAS SERIOUS . . . THEN NO ONE IS BEYOND GOD'S BLESSING.

IF YOU WANT TO BE HAPPY, stay off social media. A recent study from the University of California found that "the more you use Facebook over time, the more likely you are to experience negative physical health, negative mental health and negative life satisfaction." Psychologist Jean Twenge says it's especially harmful to young people who "look at the so-called 'highlight reels' people post on social and compare themselves, so they may feel depressed or negative emotions as a result."[1]

Of course, what gets posted on social media isn't reality. The "highlight reels" are snapshots of only the best, often inauthentic, moments. As a result, we end up comparing the unglamorous reality of our life with the fake-glamour of everyone else's. That's a recipe for despair.

While social media is a relatively recent development, the underlying human instinct to project a positive, but false, self-image is nothing new. Ancient Jewish culture was plagued by this tendency rooted in its understanding of who was #blessed. At the time of Jesus, most believed the healthy, powerful, rich, respected, and educated were clearly favored by God. The logic was simple—if your life looked good, it's because you must be good and God has blessed you for your religious devotion. The opposite was also thought to be true—if your life looked bad, it must be because you are bad and God has cursed you for your sinfulness.

Like modern social media, this desire to be perceived as blessed by God led people in Jesus' culture to project a positive, but false, public image. The truth about your life was less important than what people thought was the truth.

Jesus didn't play that game.

Instead, in His sermon, Jesus described who is really blessed—and it wasn't those who looked #blessed by the culture. New Testament scholar Scot McKnight says,

> *Clearly, Jesus goes against the grain. Instead of blessing the one who pursues wisdom and reason and develops a reputation as a sage, and instead of blessing the one who has a good family, who observes the whole Torah, or the one who has all the right friends and develops*

*a reputation as righteous or as a leader, Jesus blesses
those whom no one else blessed.*[2]

Jesus' countercultural list of who is blessed challenges us
in at least two ways. First, it means that no one is beyond God's
blessing, and even those society calls "cursed" or "worthless"
are to be shown dignity as recipients of God's care. Second,
Jesus obliterates our wicked tendency to judge others by their
circumstances. Of course, the same goes for judging ourselves.
Who is really blessed—or not blessed—cannot be determined
by a person's appearance, circumstances, or social media highlight reel.

 READ MORE **James 2:1–9; 1 Corinthians 1:26–31**

THE KINGDOM OF GOD IS NOT...

A)

B)

C)

D)

E) ALL OF THE ABOVE

3 IF JESUS WAS SERIOUS . . .
THEN HEAVEN IS ALREADY HERE.

JESUS REFERS TO HEAVEN regularly in the Sermon on the
Mount, including in the opening sentence: "Blessed are the poor
in spirit, for theirs is the kingdom of heaven." What is the kingdom of heaven? If we misunderstand what Jesus meant by this
phrase, then we are likely to misunderstand the whole sermon—
and probably Jesus Himself.

First, the kingdom of heaven is not the church. Some
assume a local congregation is a "church" but collecting all the

churches together is what constitutes God's "kingdom." But that is not what Jesus meant.

Second, the kingdom of heaven is not where God's people go after death. Jesus was not speaking about the afterlife in the Sermon on the Mount. In English, the word *heaven* carries all kinds of supernatural and spiritual meanings, but the actual word used by Jesus was plural (literally, *heavens*) and more like how we might use the word *skies* to describe the atmosphere. The air isn't a distant realm; it's all around us. Likewise, Jesus used the word *heavens* to speak of the nonphysical, invisible, but very present realm where God dwells.

Dallas Willard defined the kingdom of heaven this way: "Where what God wants done is done."[1] In other words, it is the realm where God rules and evil is powerless. Jesus announced that this kingdom was now "at hand," meaning it is within our reach. The kingdom of the heavens has broken into our world, and a new way of life is now possible. In the Sermon on the Mount, therefore, Jesus is unveiling a new ethic for those who belong to a new kind of kingdom that is not of this world.

 READ MORE **Colossians 1:9–14; Luke 17:20–21**

Scope of the
Human-Divine
Relationship
Expressed
By...

• The Psalms
• Consumer
  Christianity

HAPPY

SAD

TENDER

ANGRY

EXCITED

SCARED

4   IF JESUS WAS SERIOUS . . .
THEN WE WILL MAKE ROOM TO CRY.

IS THE CHRISTIAN LIFE only for happy-clappy people?
Where are the doubters, the grievers, and the "Where the heck
are You, God!" complainers? While a church pastor years ago,
I read a popular book at the time advocating for the best way to
operate a church. The author insisted that all weekend gather-
ings be called "Celebrations," and he said the tone of these gath-
erings should always be upbeat, energetic, and focused on the
victorious Christian life. (It's difficult to read a book that makes
your eyes roll as much as that one did.)

The problem with this nonstop celebration model, apart from being inauthentic, is the way it ignores the example found in the Bible. The book of Psalms, for instance, served as the prayer book and worship liturgy for God's ancient people. It's the prayer book Jesus and His disciples would have used in their worship. Psalms includes many songs of celebration, but there are even more prayers of lament, complaint, and even cries for justice. "How long, O LORD?" is a frequent prayer in the psalms, and it shows that the human-divine relationship has many dimensions. Ancient worship, it seems, could be celebratory, angry, mournful, repentant, or contemplative. So why do we think our worship should only be one dimensional?

Jesus said, "Blessed are those who mourn." This addresses those who are experiencing grief, but it can also include those who mourn alongside others in their pain. Where do we make space for this legitimate part of the Christian life to find expression in our communities? We must not fall into the delusion that God has called us to a perpetual state of ever-increasing happiness. Jesus reminds us that God is also with us when we mourn, and because this is a broken world mourning is to be expected. But we do not weep as those without hope.

 READ MORE **Isaiah 61:1–4; Revelation 21:3–4**

THE WAY OF
LOVE, JOY, PEACE,
PATIENCE, KINDNESS,
GOODNESS, GENTLENESS...

"WHEN THEY GO LOW WE GO HIGH."

KINGDOM
OF HEAVEN →

ZEALOTS

THE WAY OF POWER, OUTRAGE, AGGRESSION, VIOLENCE,
COERCION, DOMINATION, LIES & DIVISION.
"OUR RIGHTEOUS GOALS JUSTIFY OUR MEANS."

5   IF JESUS WAS SERIOUS . . . THEN WE WILL TRUST GOD MORE AND POLITICS LESS.

WHO ARE THE MEEK and why will they inherit the earth?
First, we must understand Jesus' context and how His audience
would have heard this statement. The word translated as "earth"
can also be translated as "land," which is probably a better reading. Throughout the Bible, the relationship between God and
His people was linked to the promised land. Faithfulness to God
meant they could dwell in the land in peace, but unfaithfulness
to God meant losing the land and being forced into exile.

Centuries before Jesus, the Jews had returned from exile to the promised land, but they did not fully possess it. The Romans, who were pagans and idolaters, ruled over the land, which was unacceptable and humiliating to the Jews. In a sense, they were still in exile because they remained under the thumb of a foreign power.

This provoked a growing number of Israelites to become Zealots—violent revolutionaries. To the Romans, the Zealots were terrorists. To many Jews, they were freedom fighters. The Zealots believed in using the world's violent ways to achieve what they believed were God's goals. Their goal was to "inherit the land" by force. By announcing that the meek were blessed and would "inherit the land," Jesus was condemning the tactics of the Zealots. He was proclaiming that it was not the powerful, violent, or angry who will accomplish God's purposes, but the gentle, peaceful, and those who put their trust in Him rather than the sword.

This is an important reminder for those of us living in a divided land where everything has become politicized between "us" and "them." Like the Zealots, we can be tempted to use the world's ways—coercion, power, and fear—to "take back the land" for God. Instead, Jesus calls us to put such things aside and discover the power of God available through meekness. It is by trusting the Lord and the meekness of His ways, not through the sword of politics, that the land is won.

 READ MORE **Zechariah 4:7; Ephesians 6:10–20**

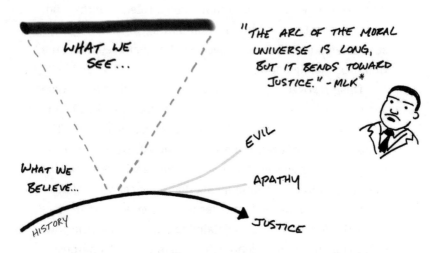

WHAT WE SEE...

"THE ARC OF THE MORAL UNIVERSE IS LONG, BUT IT BENDS TOWARD JUSTICE." - MLK*

WHAT WE BELIEVE...

HISTORY

EVIL

APATHY

JUSTICE

* MLK WAS QUOTING AN IDEA FROM A SERMON BY THEODORE PARKER.

6   IF JESUS WAS SERIOUS . . . THEN A DESIRE FOR JUSTICE SHOULD BE AFFIRMED.

"IT'S NOT FAIR!" With three kids, I hear that a lot in my household. Although the phrase is often misapplied—a fact my wife and I point out often to our apparently persecuted progeny—it does not diminish the strength of their instinct for justice. We all carry a sense that the world is not what it ought to be, and we also have a profound desire for this wrongness to be made into rightness—or what the Bible calls "righteousness."

The word is often used to describe a properly ordered

relationship between God and His people. Violating this relationship makes one unrighteous, while faithfulness to God results in a declaration of one's righteousness. The word, however, carries a much broader meaning. It can also apply to right relationships between people, between the government and the governed, and between humans and creation. That's why the same words often translated as "righteousness" in the Bible are also regularly translated in English as "justice."

Whether it is the shout for justice by a protestor or the call to be reconciled to God by a preacher, Jesus affirms our longing for justice: "Blessed are those who hunger and thirst for justice/righteousness, for they shall be satisfied." He equates the soul's desire for justice with the unrelenting physical desire for food and water. It is an inescapable aspect of our human condition, and He promises that it will be quenched. We can be assured that, in time, God will set all things right. The desire that God placed in our hearts will ultimately be satisfied. As Martin Luther King Jr. said, "The arc of the moral universe is long, but it bends toward justice."[1]

 READ MORE **Psalm 106:1–3; Luke 18:1–8**

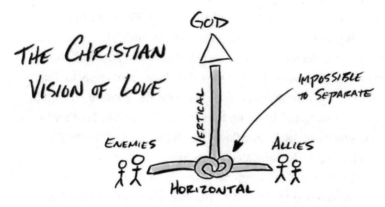

THE CHRISTIAN VISION OF LOVE

GOD

VERTICAL

IMPOSSIBLE TO SEPARATE

ENEMIES

ALLIES

HORIZONTAL

THE WAY WE SHOW OUR LOVE FOR GOD IS BY HOW WE TREAT THOSE CREATED IN HIS IMAGE. ANYONE WHO USES THEIR DEVOTION TO GOD TO JUSTIFY THEIR MISTREATMENT OF OTHERS IS A LIAR (SEE 1 JOHN 4:20).

7 IF JESUS WAS SERIOUS . . . THEN WE CANNOT SEPARATE OUR RELATIONSHIP WITH GOD FROM OUR RELATIONSHIP WITH OTHERS.

ONE OF THE RECURRING themes of Jesus' sermon is the inseparable link between our relationship with God (the vertical) and our relationship with others (the horizontal). He repeatedly emphasizes that how we treat others will determine how our heavenly Father will treat us. This idea was as uncomfortable to hear then as it is now.

For example, He said "Blessed are the merciful, for they shall receive mercy." Later, Jesus makes it clear that God's forgiveness comes with a condition—we also must forgive others (see Matt. 6:14–15). Of course, this message isn't unique to the Sermon on the Mount. It permeates the Old Testament law and the writings of the prophets, and it's carried on by Jesus' apostles.

Perhaps the reason we find this theme throughout Scripture is because the Lord knows our human inclination to separate the vertical and the horizontal. We desperately want to believe that we can stand blameless before God and utterly despise, mistreat, and condemn those created in His image. This is one of the most common and pernicious traits within religious communities. In fact, when the vertical and horizontal are completely severed, it's not uncommon for religious people to use God to justify their mistreatment of others. This is precisely what religious leaders, the Pharisees, did in Jesus' time. Those who are comfortable praising God while showing contempt for people look more like the Pharisees who killed Jesus than the disciples who followed Him.

 READ MORE **1 John 4:7–21; Isaiah 58:1–14**

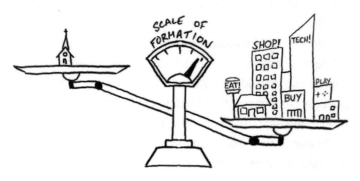

THE AVERAGE CHRISTIAN IN AMERICA...

...ATTENDS CHURCH 2 HOURS A MONTH

...IS SHAPED BY 150,000 ADS PER MONTH

SCALE OF FORMATION

SHOP! TECH! EAT! BUY PLAY

8 IF JESUS WAS SERIOUS . . . THEN OUR IMAGE ISN'T EVERYTHING.

JAY WALKER-SMITH, the president of a marketing firm, told CBS News in the 1970s that the average American was exposed to approximately five hundred ads each day. In 2006, he said it was likely as high as 5,000.[1] We are bombarded by messages and images designed to make us discontent and envious. Some worry that an ad-saturated society will make us materialistic—more occupied with possessions than with God or people. That is certainly concerning, but there is another aspect to ads we don't often consider.

In one way or another, most ads are about image—either the image of the brand being advertised or the image of the consumer the ad is targeting. In many cases, these two image identities are intertwined. While there is nothing inherently evil about marketing, absorbing thousands of image-focused ads each day can lead us to believe that our external image is all-important, and that what is beneath the surface and beyond the perception of a superficial culture is irrelevant. Simply put, ads make us think that it's what's on the outside that counts.

Long before social media marketing and algorithms, people in Jesus' culture also fixated on their external image. Of course, a person's image wasn't about brands and possessions as much as religious practices and symbols of piety. Jesus, however, dismissed the importance of the external to emphasize the internal. In God's kingdom, outward piety without inward purity is the definition of hypocrisy. This is why Jesus said, "Blessed are the pure in heart." He is more concerned with our internal posture toward God. If the heart is good, what we produce on the outside will be good as well. If our heart is wicked, no amount of image management on the outside will be enough to make us right with God.

 READ MORE **Psalm 24:3–6; Luke 11:37–52**

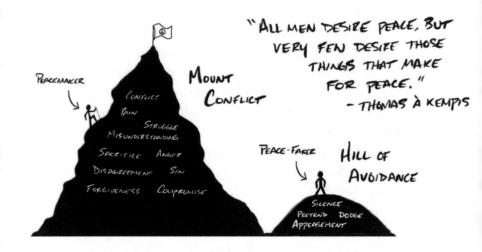

"ALL MEN DESIRE PEACE, BUT VERY FEW DESIRE THOSE THINGS THAT MAKE FOR PEACE."
— THOMAS À KEMPIS

PEACEMAKER

MOUNT CONFLICT

Conflict
Pain
Struggle
Misunderstanding
Sacrifice   Anger
Disagreement   Sin
Forgiveness   Compromise

PEACE-FAKER

HILL OF AVOIDANCE

Silence
Pretend   Dodge
Appeasement

9   IF JESUS WAS SERIOUS . . . THEN PEACE IS COSTLY BUT WORTH THE PRICE.

JESUS SAID THAT peacemakers would be "called sons of God." He did not mean this in any messianic sense. It was common in Jewish culture to use "son/sons" to attach someone to a characteristic or identity. For example, Jesus called a group of religious leaders a "brood of vipers" (Matt. 23:33) because of their lies and hypocrisy—qualities associated with snakes in the ancient world. He calls peacemakers "sons of God" because our heavenly Father is also a peacemaker, but the way God makes peace is important to recognize.

The popular perception of peacemakers, perhaps influenced by the word's negative connotation in both politics and counseling, is that of weakness and avoidance. We view peacemakers as people who desire the appearance of serenity by suppressing any visible conflict and who avoid the difficult and costly work of forging real reconciliation. Such people, however, are not peacemakers. They are peace-fakers. Avoiding conflict is not the way of God, and doing so does not make us His children.

The apostle Paul tells us that God has "reconcile[d] to himself all things . . . making peace by the blood of his cross" (Col. 1:20). Through the cross, we discover God's kind of peacemaking. It is costly and painful. Jesus forged peace not by denying the presence of evil in the world or by avoiding its power but by courageously facing it head-on. It was a hard-won peace worthy of God's praise.

What difficult circumstance or relationship are you avoiding for the sake of "peace"? Pray for the courage to do the hard, costly work of real peacemaking.

 READ MORE **Ephesians 2:11–18; Romans 12:18**

PART 2

CHRISTIANS AND CULTURE

"You are the salt of the earth, but if salt has lost its taste, how shall its saltiness be restored? It is no longer good for anything except to be thrown out and trampled under people's feet.

"You are the light of the world. A city set on a hill cannot be hidden. Nor do people light a lamp and put it under a basket, but on a stand, and it gives light to all in the house. In the same way, let your light shine before others, so that they may see your good works and give glory to your Father who is in heaven.

"Do not think that I have come to abolish the Law or the Prophets; I have not come to abolish them but to fulfill them. For truly, I say to you, until heaven and earth pass away, not an iota, not a dot, will pass from the Law until all is accomplished. Therefore whoever relaxes one of the least of these commandments and teaches others to do the same will be called least in the kingdom of heaven, but whoever does them and teaches them will be called great in the kingdom of heaven. For I tell you, unless your righteousness exceeds that of the scribes and Pharisees, you will never enter the kingdom of heaven."

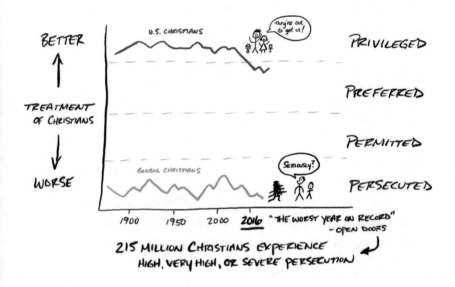

IF JESUS WAS SERIOUS . . . THEN WE WILL NOT SEE A LOSS OF PRIVILEGE AS PERSECUTION.

10

WHEN JESUS SPOKE about persecution, He made it clear that not all suffering His followers experience is persecution. He said, "Blessed are those who are persecuted for righteousness . . ." and He went on to bless those who are persecuted, "on my account." It is when we suffer for doing what is right or for being identified with Jesus that we are blessed, but there are plenty of Christians who may claim persecution who are actually suffering due to their own foolish or unrighteous behavior. Some suffer for righteousness. But frankly, some Christians suffer because they are insufferable.

"Persecution," as John Stott deftly defines it, "is simply the clash between two irreconcilable value-systems."[1] The value system presented by Jesus in the Sermon on the Mount is radically incongruent with the one presented by the world. Therefore, anyone who follows Jesus' way should expect to be misunderstood, maligned, or mistreated. In fact, persecution is often seen as a sign of genuine faith in Christ. This is why Martin Luther listed suffering as an identifying mark of the true church.

A desire to be seen as a "genuine" Christian, however, may cause us to claim persecution where none exists. This temptation is compounded by two additional realities of our age. First, the privileged position that the Christian faith and values once enjoyed in our culture is diminishing. As this occurs—for example, removing Christian prayers or symbols from public spaces—the loss of privilege can be misinterpreted as persecution.

Second, we live in a strange time when some want to claim the label of "victim" in order to accumulate cultural and political power. In other words, there can be a twisted upside to being seen as a persecuted group today. It may be used as leverage against cultural and political opponents, or to excuse one's own unrighteous attitudes and behaviors.

We must resist all of these temptations. Persecution is never something sought by a Christian. It is the by-product of seeking first the kingdom of God rather than the privileges of the world.

 READ MORE **1 Peter 2:19–25; John 15:18–27**

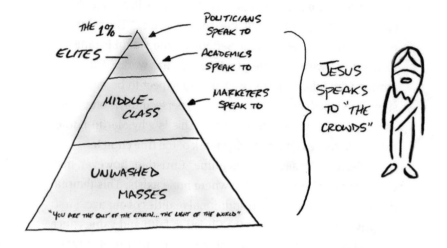

The 1% — Politicians speak to
Elites — Academics speak to
Middle-Class — Marketers speak to
Unwashed Masses
"You are the salt of the earth... the light of the world"

Jesus speaks to "the crowds"

11 IF JESUS WAS SERIOUS . . . THEN WE WILL VALUE AN ORDINARY LIFE MORE THAN A FAMOUS ONE.

WE MUST REMEMBER who Jesus addressed during His Sermon on the Mount. Matthew says Jesus was teaching the "crowds." Some translations say "the multitudes." These were the ordinary, unremarkable, some might say backward people of Galilee. Not the powerful Romans, the wise Athenians, or the religious scholars in Jerusalem. Nor was Jesus addressing the elite among His own ragtag band of students—His listeners were no one special.

Still, Jesus said to these average, ordinary people, "You are the salt of the earth. . . . You are the light of the world." It's the scope of the statement that ought to surprise us. He didn't call them the salt or light of Galilee, but the world. Forget the Caesars, and Herods, and Platos. The world doesn't need more YouTube stars or social media celebrities. Jesus affirms the world-shaping value of ordinary people who follow the ways of an extraordinary God.

It isn't that He expected each person to change the world through remarkable accomplishments. Rather, Jesus expected His undistinguished followers to be the source of the world's most essential ingredients. Pliny, who lived in the first century, commented that there is nothing more useful in the world than "salt and sunshine." Likewise, in a dark, deteriorating world, there is nothing more wonderful than simple people living as Jesus taught.

To be the salt and light of the world does not require a person to do extraordinary acts or amass spectacular influence. The world does not need more ambitious Christians. Rather, salt and light are the outcomes of ordinary lives lived in rich communion with God. Our world desperately needs more of those.

 READ MORE **2 Corinthians 5:16–17; Colossians 3:10–11**

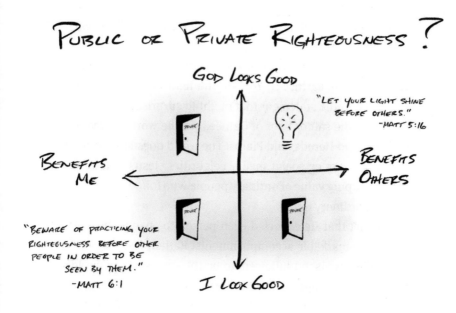

PUBLIC OR PRIVATE RIGHTEOUSNESS?

GOD LOOKS GOOD

"LET YOUR LIGHT SHINE
BEFORE OTHERS."
—MATT 5:16

**BENEFITS
ME**

**BENEFITS
OTHERS**

"BEWARE OF PRACTICING YOUR
RIGHTEOUSNESS BEFORE OTHER
PEOPLE IN ORDER TO BE
SEEN BY THEM."
—MATT 6:1

I LOOK GOOD

12 IF JESUS WAS SERIOUS . . . THEN WE WILL SEEK GOD'S GLORY RATHER THAN OUR OWN.

THERE IS A CONUNDRUM in the Sermon on the Mount. Jesus calls His followers the "light of the world." The whole purpose of a light is to provide illumination. A city on a hill cannot be hidden, Jesus said, and no one lights a lamp and then covers it. So, He commands, "Let your light shine before others, so that they may see your good works and give glory to your Father who is in heaven."

This appears to be a call to public piety—a form of religious expression that is on display for others to see. However, later in the sermon, Jesus appears to say precisely the opposite. He instructs us to do our giving in secret, to pray in private, and not to draw any attention to ourselves when fasting. How do we reconcile these seemingly contradictory calls to first a public and then a private piety? Which is it?

First, we must recognize the importance of intent. Jesus rebuked the way the other religious leaders gave, prayed, and fasted because it was clear they were seeking the approval of people. Jesus, on the other hand, calls us to "let our light shine" as a way to bring glory to God and not ourselves. We must be aware of our motives when determining whether an act should be done secretly or openly.

Second, the acts that Jesus said should remain hidden— giving, prayer, fasting—are practices of personal devotion to God. My neighbor does not benefit from my fasting, and while the poor may benefit from almsgiving, this was also primarily viewed as an act of piety toward God in the ancient world. The "good works" that Jesus compares to the preservative power of salt and the illumination of light, on the other hand, are useful things that help others.

So, we are left with these guides. If the act is for my benefit or will result in my glory, it should remain hidden. If the act is for the benefit of others and for God's glory, we should not hide it.

READ MORE **1 Peter 2:11–12; Matthew 6:1–6**

THE JUSTICE V. EVANGELISM DEBATE

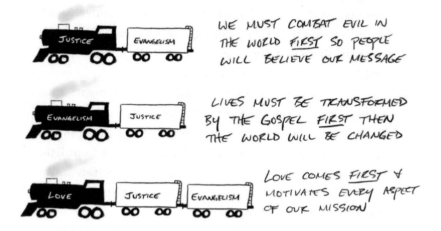

WE MUST COMBAT EVIL IN THE WORLD <u>FIRST</u> SO PEOPLE WILL BELIEVE OUR MESSAGE

LIVES MUST BE TRANSFORMED BY THE GOSPEL <u>FIRST</u> THEN THE WORLD WILL BE CHANGED

LOVE COMES <u>FIRST</u> & MOTIVATES EVERY ASPECT OF OUR MISSION

13 IF JESUS WAS SERIOUS . . . THEN BOTH EVANGELISM AND JUSTICE MATTER.

FOR DECADES, THE CHURCH in the West— and particularly in the United States—has struggled to reconcile the call to individual reconciliation with God (evangelism) with the call to social reconciliation between people (justice). A century ago, the church split over this question with more conservative Christians limiting their focus to evangelism and more progressive Christians narrowing their focus to justice. Jesus' call to His disciples to be both salt and light in the Sermon on the Mount can help us mend this division.

In the ancient world, salt was a preservative. It slowed or prevented the decay of meat, a necessity in a time before refrigeration. Light, of course, had the same function two thousand years ago as it does today. By calling us salt and light, Jesus was emphasizing two functions His followers have in the world. Like salt, we have the defensive responsibility to prevent evil—to slow or stop the decay of injustice. Like light, we also have the offensive responsibility to spread truth, goodness, and beauty—to advance the qualities of God's kingdom. In these two metaphors, John Stott saw the essential qualities of social justice and evangelism:

> *We should never put our two vocations to be salt and light, our Christian social and evangelistic responsibilities, over against each other as if we had to choose between them. We should not exaggerate either, nor disparage either, at the expense of the other. Neither can be a substitute for the other. The world needs both. It is bad and needs salt; it is dark and needs light. Our Christian vocation is to be both. Jesus Christ said so, and that should be enough.*[1]

 READ MORE **Isaiah 58:6–10; Matthew 28:17–20**

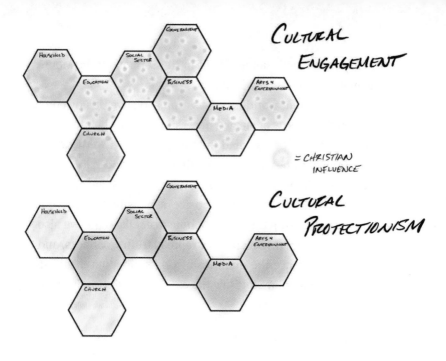

CULTURAL ENGAGEMENT

Government, Household, Social Sector, Education, Business, Arts & Entertainment, Media, Church

◯ = CHRISTIAN INFLUENCE

CULTURAL PROTECTIONISM

Government, Household, Social Sector, Education, Business, Arts & Entertainment, Media, Church

14   IF JESUS WAS SERIOUS . . . THEN WE MUST NOT WITHDRAW FROM OUR CULTURE.

WHY IS THE WORLD SO bad and who is to blame for it? Those questions occupy a lot of our attention, particularly as our society becomes more diverse and more polarized. In different eras, Christians have responded to the depravity of the world in different ways. Sometimes, the response is to flee into safe enclaves of holiness, far removed from the decay of society. This is often followed by scapegoating another community or group for society's problems.

Jesus' call to be salt and light, however, should temper our draw to either of these responses. Jesus is clear that the entire point of salt and light is to be a positive influence. A light that is covered is useless, He said. The same is true of salt that loses its preservative qualities. We cannot be salt and light if we withdraw from the darkness and decay of the world.

Rather than blaming others for the sad state of affairs and withdrawing from secular society, we ought to ask why we are so eager to withdraw in the first place. Is it a way to preserve our self-righteousness, to escape the responsibility for the world's problems? According to Jesus, this is simply not an option. We must not hide our light or keep our salt safely locked away. Rather than blaming non-Christians when things go wrong in society, we ought to start with self-reflection. Where were the Christians? How did we help, or hurt, the situation? Were we obeying our call to be salt and light?

 READ MORE **1 Peter 2:9–12; Isaiah 49:5–7**

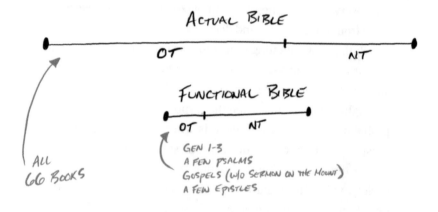

WHICH BIBLE DO YOU READ?

ACTUAL BIBLE

OT   NT

FUNCTIONAL BIBLE

OT   NT

GEN 1-3
A FEW PSALMS
GOSPELS (W/O SERMON ON THE MOUNT)
A FEW EPISTLES

ALL
66 BOOKS

15 IF JESUS WAS SERIOUS . . . THEN WE MUST ENGAGE THE OLD TESTAMENT AS WELL AS THE NEW.

EVERY CHRISTIAN HAS at least two Bibles. First, there is the actual Bible—all sixty-six books of the Old and New Testaments. Then there is the Bible we read. This is what some call our functional Bible, and it includes the sections we regularly engage and seek to apply to our lives. This functional Bible is different for each person, but it contains some familiar gospel stories and parables, some of Paul's letters, and a handful of psalms. If more people read the actual Bible, they might be very surprised by what they discover in there.

The reason many Christians have these two Bibles is because they think it is possible to grasp Jesus without needing to engage or understand the Old Testament. "That doesn't apply to us anymore," some Christians say dismissively of the Law and Prophets—the writings that came before Jesus. "All we need is what we have from Jesus and the apostles," others may think.

But that's not what Jesus said. He declared that He came not to abolish the Law and the Prophets, but to fulfill them. Fulfillment doesn't mean to finish and throw away, but to bring to completion. In other words, Jesus identifies Himself as what the Old Testament has been pointing toward, and to understand Jesus we must see Him through the lens of the writings of the Law and the Prophets. Likewise, to understand the Law and the Prophets, we must read them through the lens of Jesus. He is the key to the whole Bible, and we need the whole Bible to engage Jesus.

 READ MORE **Psalm 1:1–6; 2 Timothy 3:16–17**

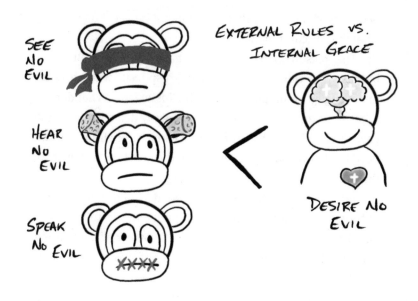

16 IF JESUS WAS SERIOUS . . . THEN THERE IS A DIFFERENCE BETWEEN DOING GOOD AND BEING GOOD.

THE PHARISEES WERE very religious men, deeply committed to the Old Testament law. In fact, they made it their mission to know, memorize, and obey every commandment of God in excruciating detail. However, when speaking about the importance of the Law, Jesus declared, "Unless your righteousness exceeds that of the scribes and Pharisees, you will never enter the kingdom of heaven." Making sense of this statement is the key to understanding what follows in the Sermon on the Mount.

While the Pharisees were mindful to obey the outward and visible commands of God's law, their righteousness went no deeper than their behavior. Jesus wasn't interested in mere external conformity. He knows that true righteousness needs to occur at the heart level. It is an internal transformation that we require, and if the inside is right, then the external behaviors will follow.

Very often in religious communities, we are content with adherence to external expectations of conduct and give little attention to the inward posture of the heart. As long as a person appears devout, uses the right words, and participates in the right religious activities, we don't look much deeper. They are often given a pass on their anger, greed, jealousy, bitterness, lust, or bigotry. Such a person might be acceptable in a church today, but Jesus said they are unfit for God's kingdom. He doesn't merely desire people who appear good, or even those who do good; He wants people who are good. That kind of inside-out transformation cannot be achieved through laws alone.

 READ MORE **Jeremiah 31:31–34; Galatians 5:16–24**

PART 3

INSIDE-OUT RIGHTEOUSNESS

"You have heard that it was said to those of old, 'You shall not murder; and whoever murders will be liable to judgment.' But I say to you that everyone who is angry with his brother will be liable to judgment; whoever insults his brother will be liable to the council; and whoever says, 'You fool!' will be liable to the hell of fire. So if you are offering your gift at the altar and there remember that your brother has something against you, leave your gift there before the altar and go. First be reconciled to your brother, and then come and offer your gift. Come to terms quickly with your accuser while you are going with him to court, lest your accuser hand you over to the judge, and the judge to the guard, and you be put in prison. Truly, I say to you, you will never get out until you have paid the last penny.

"You have heard that it was said, 'You shall not commit adultery.' But I say to you that everyone who looks at a woman with lustful intent has already committed adultery with her in his heart. If your right eye causes you to sin, tear it out and throw it away. For it is better that you lose one of your members than that your whole body be thrown into hell. And if your right hand causes you to sin, cut it off and throw it away. For it is better that you lose one of your members than that your whole body go into hell.

"It was also said, 'Whoever divorces his wife, let him give her a certificate of divorce.' But I say to you that everyone who divorces his wife, except on the ground of sexual immorality, makes her commit adultery, and whoever marries a divorced woman commits adultery.

"Again you have heard that it was said to those of old, 'You shall not swear falsely, but shall perform to the Lord what you have sworn.' But I say to you, Do not take an oath at all, either by heaven, for it is the throne of God, or by the earth, for it is his footstool, or by Jerusalem, for it is the city of the great King. And do not take an oath by your head, for you cannot make one hair white or black. Let what you say be simply 'Yes' or 'No'; anything more than this comes from evil."

3 BLIND ANGRY* MICE

* DON'T WORRY, THEY'RE RIGHTEOUS MICE

17 IF JESUS WAS SERIOUS . . . THEN WE WILL NOT CULTIVATE OUR ANGER.

SHOULD A BLIND PERSON be permitted to carry a loaded weapon? That was the focus of a 2013 court battle. Advocates for extending "Conceal and Carry" laws to include blind citizens said the visually impaired should not be discriminated against because it is the right of every American to own and carry a gun. Amazingly, the courts agreed with this argument. The case revealed a gap between legal sense and common sense.

The same gap exists regarding anger. There is biblical case

to be made for Christians wielding "righteous anger." There are many examples of God becoming angry in Scripture, including the unpopular stories of His wrath in the Old Testament, or those of Jesus overturning tables in the temple or calling down judgment upon hypocritical religious leaders in the New Testament. Since our Lord demonstrates righteous anger, shouldn't we be permitted to follow His example?

In the right hands, with the right training, and from the right heart, anger can be wielded righteously. Yet in most cases, it is only a destructive force. I rarely see all things clearly, and a weapon as dangerous as anger is best deployed only by those with perfect vision. I trust Jesus to use anger righteously. I don't trust myself. I have misfired too many times and I have hurt too many people with my anger. Adding to our misgivings about wielding anger should be Jesus' words in the Sermon on the Mount. After quoting the commandment prohibiting murder, He pivots from the external act of violence to the internal posture from which it emerges. Anger, He says, is the real problem. Is anger always wrong? No. But it is so destructive and dangerous we ought to extract it from our lives.

In prayer, admit how you've allowed anger to ferment in your mind and heart. How have you justified your anger? Are you willing to release your anger to God, who alone can be trusted to see all things clearly?

 READ MORE **Exodus 20:13; Galatians 5:16–24**

THE **NEW** FRUIT OF THE SPIRIT

(UPDATED FOR A DIGITAL GENERATION)

LOVE JOY PEACE PATIENCE KINDNESS GOODNESS OUTRAGE! FAITHFULNESS GENTLENESS SELF-CONTROL

18 IF JESUS WAS SERIOUS . . .
THEN WE WILL NOT CONTRIBUTE
TO OUR OUTRAGE CULTURE.

IT SEEMS LIKE OUR entire culture, including the church, is addicted to outrage. Anger has become the acceptable—even expected—sign of one's commitment to any cause. I have learned that if I fail to show sufficient outrage on my podcast or in a sermon, I will receive messages from other Christians who are angered by my lack of anger. They usually say, "Don't you care that . . ." somewhere in the tweet, post, or email. I sometimes feel that my credibility as a Christian depends on my willingness to brandish my anger. In some Christian communities, particularly online, anger is so ubiquitous one might suspect it is a fruit of the Spirit. Why has it found such acceptance among us when Jesus warned so clearly of anger's toxicity to our soul?

Perhaps our constant media consumption has deadened our ability to feel the more subtle human emotions. In this overstimulated environment, only the sledgehammer of anger is able to get our attention; if we don't use it to convey every emotion, we are dismissed for not having emotions at all. Or maybe we are collectively in the second stage of grieving our loss of cultural significance as the church in North America. The first phase was denial, in which we rejected the evidence of declining church attendance and cultural marginalization—a few Pollyannas are still in this first phase of grief. Many of us have now moved to the second phase: anger.

If our attraction to anger is a part of a collective grieving process, then eventually I expect we will move on to bargaining, depression, and finally acceptance that our time of cultural power has passed. Until then, we must look for ways to resist the temptation to join the advocates of outrage.

 READ MORE **James 1:19–20; Psalm 37:8–9**

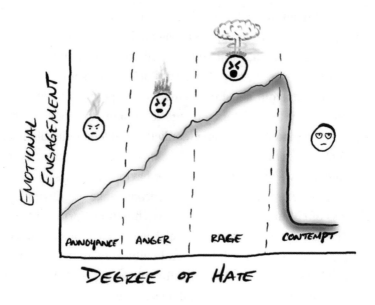

EMOTIONAL ENGAGEMENT

ANNOYANCE | ANGER | RAGE | CONTEMPT

DEGREE OF HATE

19 IF JESUS WAS SERIOUS . . . THEN WE WILL RECOGNIZE EVERY PERSON AS VALUABLE.

IN THE SERMON on the Mount, Jesus identified anger as the posture of the heart that leads to murder; it is the seed of sin that leads to the most destructive acts, therefore it must be removed from within us. Perhaps you are not an ill-tempered person—maybe you do not fly off the handle or rage when your will is frustrated. A calm demeanor, however, is not necessarily evidence that your heart is right.

Jesus spoke about a different, even more virulent form of

anger—contempt. His warning about insulting others is often passed over by modern readers as unimportant. That is a serious mistake. The insulting word He used was *raca*, a dismissive term of contempt in His culture that is derived from the sound of clearing spit from one's throat. This kind of contempt is different than mere anger. Contempt seeks to diminish the inherent value of the other person. It views the other as subhuman, not even worthy of my anger. It excludes the other person from being worthy of care, thought, or dignity.

In our culture, it is all too common to devalue those with different political values, ethnic backgrounds, sexuality, economic status, or religious traditions. In fact, many of our political and media leaders build their audiences by doing this. Of course, we should be wise and discerning, but we must not allow our loyalty to a certain group or set of ideas to breed contempt for those who disagree with us.

Justice Antonin Scalia, who died in 2016, was celebrated by conservatives and dreaded by progressives. Both sides recognized his brilliance and his sharpness of tongue and pen. Yet he was also beloved even by his opponents. It may have been because Scalia held his beliefs without contempt for his opponents. He said, "I attack ideas. I don't attack people. And some very good people have some very bad ideas. And if you can't separate the two, you gotta get another day job."[1] More of us, no matter our beliefs, should emulate his example.

 READ MORE **Luke 6:37–38; Romans 12:14–21**

WHO ARE THE "INVISIBLE" IN YOUR COMMUNITY?

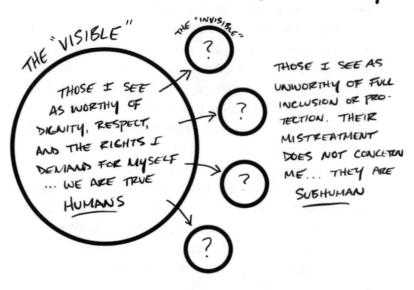

THE "VISIBLE"

THOSE I SEE AS WORTHY OF DIGNITY, RESPECT, AND THE RIGHTS I DEMAND FOR MYSELF ... WE ARE TRUE HUMANS

THE "INVISIBLE"

? ? ? ?

THOSE I SEE AS UNWORTHY OF FULL INCLUSION OR PROTECTION. THEIR MISTREATMENT DOES NOT CONCERN ME... THEY ARE SUBHUMAN

20 IF JESUS WAS SERIOUS . . . THEN NO ONE SHOULD BE INVISIBLE.

WE ALL REMEMBER that one kid in elementary school who misbehaved in class. Maybe you were that kid. I recall my teacher telling us not to respond to Bob because "he's just looking for attention." It never worked. How could anyone expect eight-year-olds to ignore Bob when he removed his glass eye and put it in his mouth? You could love Bob or hate Bob, but ignoring Bob was not an option.

Our elementary school experiences reveal a truth that Jesus

communicated in the Sermon on the Mount. Cultivating anger toward a person is dangerous, but having contempt for someone is even worse—its goal is ignoring the person altogether. In *The Divine Conspiracy*, Dallas Willard explained why this kind of contempt is worse than ordinary anger:

> *In anger I want to hurt you. In contempt, I don't care whether you are hurt or not. Or at least so I say. You are not worthy of consideration one way or the other. We can be angry at someone without denying their worth. But contempt makes it easier for us to hurt them or see them further degraded.[1]*

This kind of contemptuous dehumanization precedes every terrible atrocity. For example, the Nazis described Jews as *Untermenschen*, or subhumans. In his exploration of the Holocaust, David Livingstone Smith concluded the Nazis "didn't mean [Jews] were *like* subhumans. They meant they were *literally* subhumans."[2] Once Jews were excluded from the moral category of being human, any behavior toward them became acceptable.

When we carry contempt for another person, we believe they are unworthy of our attention, even our negative attention. Instead, they become invisible to us, mere background objects to be neither hated nor loved, and if they interfere with our goals they should be disposed of like unwanted pests. Any heart that feels so indifferent toward those created in God's image cannot be suitable for God's kingdom. No one is ever invisible to our heavenly Father. No one is unworthy of His attention.

 READ MORE **Mark 10:46–52; Hebrews 4:13**

INTERNAL V. EXTERNAL RIGHTEOUSNESS

GUARDRAILS ARE GOOD BUT BECOMING A DRIVER WHO DOES NOT NEED THEM IS BETTER.

21 IF JESUS WAS SERIOUS . . . THEN WE WILL NEED MORE THAN RULES TO BECOME GODLY.

THE TEN COMMANDMENTS and the entire Old Testament law can be seen as a set of guardrails on the behavior of God's people. Like other ancient societies, Israel was also plagued by cycles of violence and revenge and corrosive hedonism, so the Lord gave His people commands to limit these forces and to ensure Israel's flourishing. By obeying His laws, they could avoid careening off the road into destruction like so many other ancient societies.

The seventh commandment against adultery served this purpose. By honoring the covenant of marriage, the people created the necessary conditions for social stability and growth; stable households provided safety and economic security for women and children. The law forbidding adultery wasn't just a matter of personal morality, but one of social security. It was a guardrail to keep the entire community on the road to a flourishing future.

But guardrails are never enough. While they may keep an out-of-control driver from going over a cliff, guardrails alone will never teach us to drive like Mario Andretti.

Jesus affirmed the seventh commandment against adultery in the Sermon on the Mount, but then He said, "Everyone who looks at a woman with lustful intent has already committed adultery with her in his heart." Jesus isn't merely interested in good behavior; He wants us to be good people. After all, a person with excellent driving skills and complete control of the car doesn't need guardrails.

Are you just focused on staying within the lines, obeying the rules, and avoiding a wreck? Or have you come to see the limits of guardrails?

 READ MORE **Proverbs 6:20–29; Exodus 20:14**

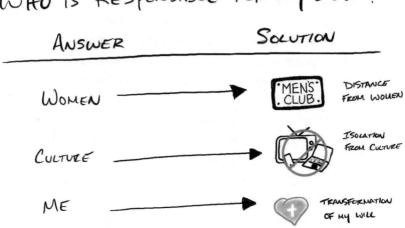

WHO IS RESPONSIBLE FOR MY LUST?

ANSWER | SOLUTION

WOMEN → MEN'S CLUB — DISTANCE FROM WOMEN

CULTURE → ISOLATION FROM CULTURE

ME → TRANSFORMATION OF MY WILL

22 IF JESUS WAS SERIOUS . . . THEN LUST IS A CHOICE.

IN CASE YOU HAVEN'T noticed, we live in a sex-saturated society. The church has tended to offer two responses to this fact—condemnation or accommodation. Condemnation is both a simplification and often an overreaction. It merely says, "Sexual immorality is bad." This posture seeks to protect Christians from the cultural idolatry of desire, but it often does more harm than good because it offers no healthy, alternative model of sexuality for us to follow.

Accommodation, on the other hand, affirms the cultural narrative that desires cannot be controlled, that we are all rudderless ships being carried along by sexual currents far beyond our power to resist. As access to sexually explicit material has multiplied, so has the accommodation viewpoint within the church.

Both condemnation and accommodation assume we are passive victims of desire, and both place all of the blame for our struggle "out there" in the culture, but Jesus' words in the Sermon on the Mount offer a more nuanced view. He said, "Everyone who looks at a woman with lustful intent has already committed adultery with her in his heart." The translation is important. Some English versions omit the word "intent," which has led some to think that looking at any woman, at any time, and in any manner is sinful or automatically leads to lustful thoughts. In truth, lust is a choice. It is something we intend. If chosen frequently enough, it can become a compulsive response that bypasses our conscious will, but it does not begin that way.

Jesus does not condemn sexual desires even when those desires are provoked by unexpected or unwelcome temptations, and He does not place the blame for lust on women, the culture, or any other external force. Rather, He warns about the deformation that happens when we deliberately engage our will in the pursuit of lust.

 READ MORE **2 Timothy 2:22; James 1:13–15**

YES, JESUS USED HUMOR & HYPERBOLE

"DID YOU HEAR ABOUT THE MUTILATED STUMP THAT ROLLED INTO HEAVEN?"

23 IF JESUS WAS SERIOUS . . . THEN WE WILL TAKE SIN IN OUR LIVES SERIOUSLY.

ONE OF THE MORE confounding parts of the Sermon on the Mount is where Jesus speaks of tearing out your eye and cutting off your hand if they cause you to sin. "For it is better that you lose one of your members than that your whole body be thrown into hell." What does that mean?

Over the centuries, some have taken His words literally and prescribed self-mutilation to avoid sin. Thankfully, most scholars agree that Jesus was using hyperbole, but they disagree about how we are to understand this teaching. Some read His words, although exaggerated, as deadly serious. Oswald Chambers, for example, read this as a call to "stern discipline" in the pursuit of holiness by "cutting off a great many things for the sake of one's spiritual life."[1]

Others, however, read Jesus' words as rabbinical sarcasm not meant to be taken seriously at all. Dallas Willard, for example, saw the call to pluck out eyes and cut off hands as Jesus' way of showing the logical and absurd end of the religious focus on external law-keeping. He wrote,

> In [the Pharisees'] view, the law could be satisfied, and thus goodness attained, if you avoided sinning.... You could avoid sinning if you simply eliminated the bodily parts that make sinful actions possible. Then you would roll into heaven a mutilated stump.
>
> ... But so far from suggesting that any advantage could actually be gained in this way, Jesus' teaching in this passage is exactly the opposite. The mutilated stump could still have a wicked heart.... Eliminating bodily parts will not change that.[2]

So what are we to make of Jesus' teaching? However one reads it—as serious or sarcastic—there is a truth to apply. If our hearts are transformed, as Willard says is necessary, the transformation will be manifested in new behaviors, including the practice of "stern discipline," as Chambers writes, in the avoidance of sin. What we must avoid is the error of thinking holiness is either an external or an internal reality: it must transform both our intent and our actions.

 READ MORE **Hebrews 12:1–4; Psalm 119:6–16**

PART 4

LOVE
IN ACTION

"You have heard that it was said, 'An eye for an eye and a tooth for a tooth.' But I say to you, Do not resist the one who is evil. But if anyone slaps you on the right cheek, turn to him the other also. And if anyone would sue you and take your tunic, let him have your cloak as well. And if anyone forces you to go one mile, go with him two miles. Give to the one who begs from you, and do not refuse the one who would borrow from you.

"You have heard that it was said, 'You shall love your neighbor and hate your enemy.' But I say to you, Love your enemies and pray for those who persecute you, so that you may be sons of your Father who is in heaven. For he makes his sun rise on the evil and on the good, and sends rain on the just and on the unjust. For if you love those who love you, what reward do you have? Do not even the tax collectors do the same? And if you greet only your brothers, what more are you doing than others? Do not even the Gentiles do the same? You therefore must be perfect, as your heavenly Father is perfect."

THE NARCISSIST LOVES ONLY HIMSELF.

THE NATIONALIST LOVES ONLY HIS TRIBE.

THE ACTIVIST LOVES ONLY HIS CAUSE.

THE IDEALIST LOVES ONLY HIS THOUGHTS.

THE HUMANIST LOVES ONLY HIS CONCEPT
OF HUMANITY.

THE CHRISTIAN LOVES THE IRRITATING
PERSON RIGHT IN FRONT OF HIM.

 24

IF JESUS WAS SERIOUS . . . THEN WE WILL LOVE THE PEOPLE WHO ANNOY US EVERY DAY.

WE TEND PUT PEOPLE into two categories—friends and enemies. Those we like and those we don't. People who are with us and people who are against us. Hopefully, most Christians recoil at the idea of hating anyone. We've been taught to love our neighbors and we may even give lip service to the call to love our enemies. There is a significant difference, however, between affirming these noble ideas and actually living them.

In *The Brothers Karamazov*, Fyodor Dostoyevsky wrote

about the ease of loving "humanity" while hating actual humans:

> *The more I love humanity in general, the less I love man in particular. In my dreams, I have often come to making enthusiastic schemes for the service of humanity, and perhaps I might actually have faced crucifixion if it had been suddenly necessary; and yet I am incapable of living in the same room with anyone for two days together, as I know by experience. As soon as anyone is near me, his personality disturbs my self-complacency and restricts my freedom. In twenty-four hours I begin to hate the best of men: one because he's too long over his dinner; another because he has a cold and keeps on blowing his nose. I become hostile to people the moment they come close to me. But it has always happened that the more I detest men individually the more ardent becomes my love for humanity.*[1]

In the Sermon on the Mount, Jesus is calling us to love the everyday enemies in our own households—the annoying humans who interfere with our wills and obstruct our desires with mundane regularity. That means loving the inconsiderate spouse, the self-centered teenager, and the absent-minded child. It is a call to love the disrespectful boss and the demanding client. Take a moment to identify the "enemies" in your life, those you struggle to love, and ask for the grace to love them today.

 READ MORE **Exodus 23:4–5; Romans 5:6–11**

What God Said	v.	What People Hear
Love your Neighbor — Lev 19:18		Hate your Enemy
God Created the Heavens & the Earth — Gen 1:1		Science is a Lie
Do not Oppress an Immigrant — Ex 23:9		Do not Oppress a Documented Immigrant
God is Love — 1 Jn 4:8		God Agrees with Me & I Don't Have to Change

25 IF JESUS WAS SERIOUS . . . THEN WE WILL VALUE GOD'S WORDS MORE THAN OUR TRADITIONS.

"YOU HAVE HEARD that it was said . . ." Jesus uses this phrase a number of times in the Sermon on the Mount before introducing a new topic. In each case, it is followed by a commandment from the Old Testament. For example, "You have heard that it was said, 'You shall love your neighbor and hate your enemy.'" While the Old Testament law does command God's people to love their neighbor, nowhere does it command them to hate their enemies. In fact, there are numerous texts in the Old Testament that tell people to have love or mercy on their enemies (see Gen. 45; Ex. 23:4; 1 Sam. 24:7; 2 Kings 6:22; Prov. 25:21). So why does Jesus link these two commands together?

It appears to be a case of inference. When God's people heard the command "love your neighbor," they incorrectly assumed the inverse—don't love the person who is not your neighbor. Over time, this became codified as "hate your enemy," a command that appears nowhere in the Bible, but one that many people assume. Jesus rejected this false assumption. Instead, He called the people to love their neighbors and their enemies.

We still see this tendency to infer negative applications of God's good commands today. For example, the good call to "go and make disciples" does not mean we should devalue other important tasks undertaken by Christ's followers. Affirming the good Christian ethic of marriage does not justify demonizing or persecuting those with a different understanding. Holding to the authority of Scripture does not mean all other sources of truth—including science—are illegitimate.

Very often, what gets Christians into trouble is not holding to God's commands, but stridently holding to the assumptions we've inferred from God's commands.

 READ MORE **Mark 3:1–6; Galatians 6:1–3**

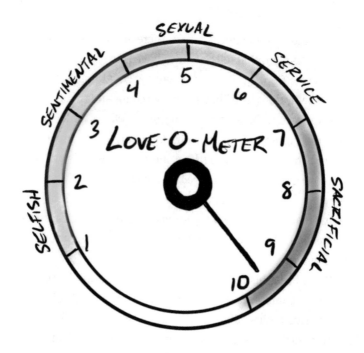

26 IF JESUS WAS SERIOUS . . . THEN WE WILL LOVE WITH OUR ACTIONS, NOT MERELY OUR FEELINGS.

"GOD IS LOVE." IT'S one of the most quoted sentences in the New Testament. There is a great gap, however, between what the apostle John meant when he wrote it and how we often hear it. The word "love" carries a lot of cultural baggage. Modern, Western people hear "love" and conjure up ideas of romantic infatuation, gooey feelings, and sweet sentimentality. We think of love as a soft, gentle emotion.

counterintuitive commands appear more conventional or at least less ridiculous. Behind this is really a desire to justify ourselves. We desperately want to rationalize our hatred and anger. We want to retaliate and resist those who interfere with our desires. We want to believe our selfishness and devotion to self-preservation are not only acceptable but admirable qualities for a Christian.

Jesus, however, leaves no room for such arguments. The ethic of love that dominates His kingdom is all-encompassing. Our call to self-sacrificial love must override and restrain our instinct for retaliation.

Rather than reading these statements in the Sermon on the Mount as commands or laws to be obeyed, we ought to see them as illustrations of a life shaped by God's kingdom. They are examples of what happens when we consider what is best for the other person rather than ourselves, even if that other person is our enemy.

 READ MORE **1 Peter 2:18–25; Isaiah 50:6–9**

PRAY FOR YOUR ENEMY. YOU WON'T SEE HIM THE SAME WAY.

28   IF JESUS WAS SERIOUS . . . THEN PRAYER WILL TRANSFORM HOW WE SEE OUR ENEMIES.

JESUS TELLS US TO love our enemies and pray for them. These are not two different commands. The former is fulfilled, at least in part, by the latter. To love a person is to seek what is good for him. What greater good can there be than to ask for God's favor upon the one who hates us?

But I believe Jesus had another reason for commanding us to pray for our enemies. He understands that we cannot genuinely pray for another and continue to hate him. In prayer, our vision of the person is transformed as we see him in the light of God's presence. Dietrich Bonhoeffer wrote about the reorienting power of prayer within Christian communities (where a great many of our enemies are often found):

> *A Christian community either lives by the intercessory prayers of its members for one another, or the community will be destroyed. I can no longer condemn or hate other Christians for whom I pray, no matter how much trouble they cause me. In intercessory prayer the face that may have been strange and intolerable to me is transformed into the face of one for whom Christ died, the face of a pardoned sinner. That is a blessed discovery for the Christian who is beginning to offer intercessory prayer for others. As far as we are concerned, there is no dislike, no personal tension, no disunity or strife that cannot be overcome by intercessory prayer. Intercessory prayer is the purifying bath into which the individual and the community must enter every day.*[1]

 READ MORE **Luke 23:33–34; 1 Peter 3:8–9**

PART 5

A PRAYER
FOR LOSERS

"Beware of practicing your righteousness before other people in order to be seen by them, for then you will have no reward from your Father who is in heaven.

"Thus, when you give to the needy, sound no trumpet before you, as the hypocrites do in the synagogues and in the streets, that they may be praised by others. Truly, I say to you, they have received their reward. But when you give to the needy, do not let your left hand know what your right hand is doing, so that your giving may be in secret. And your Father who sees in secret will reward you.

"And when you pray, you must not be like the hypocrites. For they love to stand and pray in the synagogues and at the street corners, that they may be seen by others. Truly, I say to you, they have received their reward. But when you pray, go into your room and shut the door and pray to your Father who is in secret. And your Father who sees in secret will reward you.

"And when you pray, do not heap up empty phrases as the Gentiles do, for they think that they will be heard for their many words. Do not be like them, for your Father knows what you need before you ask him. Pray then like this:

> "Our Father in heaven,
> hallowed be your name.
> Your kingdom come,
> your will be done,
>> on earth as it is in heaven.
> Give us this day our daily bread,
> and forgive us our debts,
>> as we also have forgiven our debtors.
> And lead us not into temptation,
>> but deliver us from evil.

For if you forgive others their trespasses, your heavenly Father will also forgive you, but if you do not forgive others their trespasses, neither will your Father forgive your trespasses."

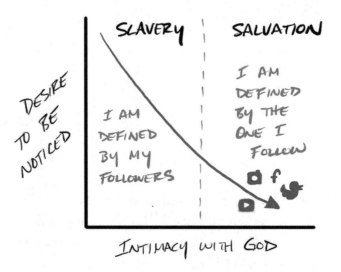

SALVATION FROM SOCIAL MEDIA

SLAVERY | SALVATION

DESIRE TO BE NOTICED

I AM DEFINED BY MY FOLLOWERS

I AM DEFINED BY THE ONE I FOLLOW

INTIMACY WITH GOD

29 IF JESUS WAS SERIOUS . . . THEN WE WILL VALUE INTIMACY MORE THAN PUBLICITY.

IN 2016, MUMBAI, INDIA, established sixteen "no selfie zones" across the city after a series of deadly accidents. Mumbai is not alone. *The Washington Post* has reported that over 250 people have died in recent years while attempting to take selfies. (Which seems low to me.) The data says drowning is the most common cause of selfie-death, followed by vehicles, falling, firearms, animal attacks, and electrocution.[1] It appears our desire to be seen by others is killing us.

We all want our lives to matter, but in our celebrity-saturated culture, we've come to believe that our lives matter only if they are noticed. This deep longing to matter by being seen is what fuels social media. We want someone, anyone, to take notice, to care about us, to see us and like us. We go online to find a witness to our life, but what we're really searching for on Facebook, Instagram, and Twitter is someone to tell us, "You matter. Your life counts."

In this selfie-culture, we must hear Jesus' reminder that what is done in secret is what matters most. Real intimacy—whether with another person or God—requires privacy and shuns publicity. This is why Jesus calls us to conduct our charity, our fasting, and our praying without being noticed by others. God is to be our only witness because He has become our only desire. "And your Father who sees in secret will reward you."

The more we develop this intimacy with God, the less we will strive for the affirmation and attention of others—including strangers via social media. We will also discover a secret that eludes so many: our lives do matter. Not because someone noticed our post and "liked" it, but because God is always with us, noticing every moment of our lives. He knows when I sit and when I rise; He knows my thoughts from afar. He discerns my going out and my lying down, as well as every word on my tongue before I say it.

 READ MORE **Psalm 139:1–12; 1 Corinthians 4:1–5**

30 IF JESUS WAS SERIOUS . . . THEN WE ARE NEVER TRULY ALONE WHEN WE PRAY.

IN THE MIDDLE OF the Sermon on the Mount, we find the most well-known passage in the Bible: the Lord's Prayer. Long before most people had access to the Bible, and well before most people were educated enough to read it, they were taught the Lord's Prayer. It has been used in Christian worship since the beginning of the church and continues to be a guide for how we commune individually and corporately with God.

Jesus taught us to pray by addressing God as "Our Father."

The Lord's Prayer is not a private prayer. Nowhere do the pronouns "I," "me," or "my" appear here. Only "our" and "us." The prayer of Jesus assumes we are connected—that we are part of a community. Individualism is a foundation of Western culture. In our minds, independence not only means freedom from oppression but freedom from other people altogether. But this American value is not part of Jesus' teachings. Christian prayer, even when done alone, is never really a private activity. We are forever connected to one another—and God intended it to be that way.

We all are part of the great family of God that transcends every boundary: national, ethnic, cultural, even generational. When we bow our heads and pray these words, we are taking part in a family prayer. The Lord's Prayer binds the people of God together across time and space.

Today, as you commune with God in silence and in prayer, recite the Lord's Prayer silently or aloud. As you say the plural pronouns "our" and "us," pay attention to the faces that come into your mind. Remember your sisters and your brothers. Remember that we all share the same Father in heaven and that your communion with Him cannot be separated from your communion with them.

 READ MORE **Romans 8:12–17; Ephesians 4:1–6**

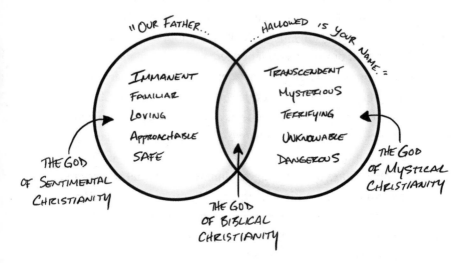

INTIMATE FATHER & HOLY OTHER

"OUR FATHER...

HALLOWED IS YOUR NAME. =

IMMANENT
FAMILIAR
LOVING
APPROACHABLE
SAFE

TRANSCENDENT
MYSTERIOUS
TERRIFYING
UNKNOWABLE
DANGEROUS

THE GOD
OF SENTIMENTAL
CHRISTIANITY

THE GOD
OF MYSTICAL
CHRISTIANITY

THE GOD
OF BIBLICAL
CHRISTIANITY

31   IF JESUS WAS SERIOUS . . . THEN GOD IS BOTH TENDER AND TERRIFYING.

THE PRAYER THAT Jesus taught His followers begins with "Our Father in heaven." Jesus quickly contrasts the intimate closeness of "Our Father" with God's transcendent holiness. The second phrase says "hallowed be your name." To call God's name hallowed is to say our Father is Himself holy. We often think of holy as meaning "morally pure or good," but the word actually means "separate, set apart, or utterly different." When we pray "hallowed be your name," we are saying our God is unlike anything else—He is beyond anything in the universe, beyond our ability to fully grasp. The writer of Hebrews calls Him a "consuming fire," beautiful and dangerous. We are attracted to Him, yet find Him utterly unapproachable.

This prayer of Jesus establishes a paradox between our accessible heavenly Father—who is an intimate caregiver—and the unapproachable Holy One in heaven—who is entirely unlike us, or anything else we might imagine.

How can our God be both our intimate Father and a holy fire? How can He be both tender and terrifying? The temptation is to see only one side, to ignore what we don't understand or what we find unappealing, and choose to see only part of who God is. In doing this, we create a new god—a false god of our own creation and in our own image.

Jesus invites us into true prayer with the true God. This kind of prayer must start with a true vision of who God is—as incomprehensible as that vision may be. Rather than comprehend Him, we are invited to cease our pondering and fall down in worship before the God who is a holy bonfire of love. Only such a God is worthy of my prayer because any god I can fully understand can be no greater than myself.

 READ MORE **Revelation 4:8–11; Hebrews 12:28–29**

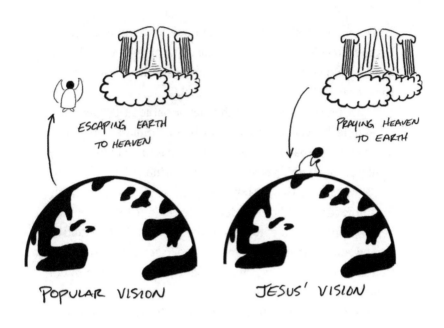

ESCAPING EARTH
TO HEAVEN

PRAYING HEAVEN
TO EARTH

POPULAR VISION

JESUS' VISION

32 IF JESUS WAS SERIOUS . . . THEN WE WILL WANT TO TRANSFORM THE EARTH NOT ESCAPE TO HEAVEN.

OLIVER WENDELL HOLMES famously said, "Some people are so heavenly minded that they are no earthly good."[1] Sadly, this description could apply to many Christians who have uncritically accepted the notion that this world does not ultimately matter to God, and therefore should not matter to us. "We're just passing through" and "This world is not my home" are popular clichés among followers of Christ today.

This dismissive posture toward the world does not align with how Jesus taught us to pray. After addressing God as both our intimate Father and as holy Other, we pray, "Your kingdom come, your will be done, on earth as it is in heaven." This is the great desire and aspiration of all who belong to God. Rather than praying to escape the earth for heaven, Jesus tells us to pray for God's kingdom to arrive on earth from heaven.

Like much of the Lord's Prayer, this phrase carries both a longing and a responsibility. First, we long to see our world bloom with the order, beauty, and abundance that marks God's kingdom, and we want every ounce of injustice, death, and scarcity purged away. This full hope will only be fulfilled when the power of Jesus' resurrection is unleashed throughout the cosmos in the age to come.

Second, however, is the implied responsibility upon all who would utter this prayer. In longing for God's will to be done on the earth, we are affirming a surrender of our wills to God's. We are making ourselves servants of God's kingdom on earth rather than expecting God to serve our kingdoms.

 READ MORE **Matthew 26:36–39; Luke 1:34–38**

"GIVE US THIS DAY...

INSTRUCTIONS: CONNECT THE PRAYER TO THE ONE WHO PRAYED IT.

THE LORD'S PRAYER

THE PROSPERITY PRAYER

THE ATHEIST'S PRAYER

THE WORRIER'S PRAYER

THE ACTIVIST'S PRAYER

THE JEALOUS PRAYER

... OUR BREAD FOR TOMORROW."

... OUR NEIGHBOR'S BREAD."

... ENOUGH BREAD TO RETIRE, AND A BMW."

... NEVERMIND. WE'LL GET OUR OWN BREAD."

... ONLY LOCALLY SOURCED, ORGANIC, NON-GMO BREAD."

... OUR DAILY BREAD."

33 IF JESUS WAS SERIOUS . . . THEN WE WILL BE CONTENT TO HAVE WHAT WE NEED FOR TODAY.

IN OUR COMMUNION with God, Jesus invites us to pray: "Give us this day our daily bread." This simple request shows that a life with God is one of ongoing, unending, daily dependence. In other words, it is a life of faith.

We may take "bread" literally to mean food or it may represent everything that is required to sustain our life. Limiting the request to our daily bread means seeking only enough for today. Today, Jesus calls us to trust our heavenly Father for today, and we are invited to trust Him anew tomorrow. By doing this, we reject the world's frenzied, fearful drive to accumulate and hoard. Fear drives us to seek control. Love compels us to trust.

Has it ever occurred to you that Jesus never hurried? There is no record in the Gospels of Jesus rushing or worrying. He trusted that His Father would provide for Him, and He expected this kind of faith of His followers.

When we live the Lord's Prayer, we learn to let go of our rushing; we learn to release our fear of not having enough and our striving for control. We begin to slow down, trust our Father, and discover that true life is not found in what we eat or drink or wear or drive.

What an incredible challenge for us. In one of the wealthiest, most fed cultures that has ever existed, will we hear Jesus ask, "Will you be content with enough bread for today? Will you slow down? Will you release the worries of this world and find your true life in communion with God?"

 READ MORE **Matthew 6:30–33; John 6:35–51**

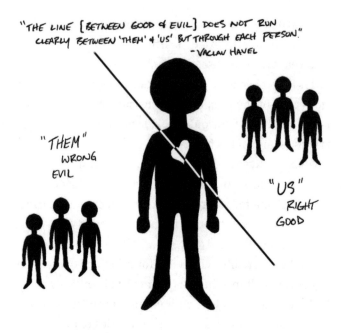

"THE LINE [BETWEEN GOOD & EVIL] DOES NOT RUN CLEARLY BETWEEN 'THEM' & 'US' BUT THROUGH EACH PERSON."
— VACLAV HAVEL

"THEM"
WRONG
EVIL

"US"
RIGHT
GOOD

34   IF JESUS WAS SERIOUS . . . THEN WE WILL SEE THE EVIL IN US NOT MERELY THE EVIL IN OTHERS.

THE LORD'S PRAYER is more than simply an example of how to speak to God. As each phrase of this prayer builds on the previous, Jesus reveals profound truths about how a life with God is lived. For example, if we do not see God properly as both heavenly Father and holy Other (Matt. 6:9), we will not surrender ourselves to His will (Matt. 6:10). Our un-surrendered life easily falls victim to the fears of the world, and we will strive to secure our own daily bread (Matt. 6:11). A hurried, fearful, selfish life fueled by a false vision of God will inevitably lead to sin—and the need for forgiveness. "Forgive us our debts, as we also have forgiven our debtors" (Matt. 6:12).

Jesus knows that our souls need forgiveness as surely as our bodies need bread, but receiving forgiveness is not enough. A healthy soul must also give it. Holding to our anger and resentment, clinging to our identity as a victim, and refusing to release others from their debts will leave us incapable of receiving God's love—or anyone else's.

In Jesus' prayer, it is important to see that sin is not merely an external opponent to be overcome nor infractions committed by others against us that must be forgiven. Sin is also an internal reality we must acknowledge about ourselves. Vaclav Havel, former president of the Czech Republic, said, "The line [between good and evil] does not run clearly between 'them' and 'us,' but through each person."[1]

As we recite these words from the Lord's Prayer, it is appropriate to pause for self-reflection and invite the Spirit of God to reveal how we have wronged God and others by what we have done, and by what we have left undone.

 READ MORE **Colossians 3:12–14; Psalm 130:1–4**

"LEAD US..."

TEMPTATION
GOD'S KINGDOM
EVIL
GOOD

35 · IF JESUS WAS SERIOUS . . . THEN WE WILL ADMIT OUR INABILITY TO RESCUE OURSELVES. .

JESUS CONCLUDES His prayer, "Lead us not into temptation, but deliver us from evil." For those living with God—for those who have tasted His goodness—there will arise an unceasing desire for deliverance from sin and evil. The ultimate goal, however, is not simply the removal of sin from our lives. Too often, we forget that our God doesn't merely deliver us from something. He also delivers us to something.

The writer of Hebrews tells us to fix our eyes on Jesus and put aside the sin that so easily entangles us (Heb. 12:1–2). Sin is like thorny brush that slows us from reaching and embracing our treasure. This fact is lost if we do not see the Lord's Prayer as a single, developing thought. To be delivered from evil means being delivered into the unmediated presence of our heavenly Father. We want to overcome temptation because we are overjoyed with God. He is our treasure. Separating these two ideas does great damage to our life with God and our growth as His people.

When we pray, "Lead us not into temptation," we are also admitting to God that we do not have the strength to rescue ourselves. We are saying, "Lead me because I cannot lead myself." Ray Pritchard has said this part of the Lord's Prayer is intended for pathetic losers, but we shouldn't be discouraged, because that includes all of us. He writes, "Without God we don't have a chance, we don't have a thing to offer, and we don't even know what to do next."[1]

In the Old Testament, there is another prayer that models this need for guidance. When a massive army came against King Jehoshaphat, he turned to God with this prayer:

> "O, LORD, God of our fathers, are you not God in heaven? You rule over all the kingdoms of the nations. In your hand are power and might, so that none is able to withstand you. . . . O our God, will you not execute judgment on them? For we are powerless against this great horde that is coming against us. We do not know what to do, but our eyes are on you." (2 Chron. 20:6, 12)

When you pray, begin your time with God by admitting your weakness and humbly asking for God's guidance—not just to lead you away from sin, but into His presence.

 READ MORE **Hebrews 12:1–2; 2 Chronicles 20:6–12**

PART 6

FREEDOM FROM FEAR

"And when you fast, do not look gloomy like the hypocrites, for they disfigure their faces that their fasting may be seen by others. Truly, I say to you, they have received their reward. But when you fast, anoint your head and wash your face, that your fasting may not be seen by others but by your Father who is in secret. And your Father who sees in secret will reward you.

"Do not lay up for yourselves treasures on earth, where moth and rust destroy and where thieves break in and steal,but lay up for yourselves treasures in heaven, where neither moth nor rust destroys and where thieves do not break in and steal. For where your treasure is, there your heart will be also.

"The eye is the lamp of the body. So, if your eye is healthy, your whole body will be full of light, but if your eye is bad, your whole body will be full of darkness. If then the light in you is darkness, how great is the darkness!

"No one can serve two masters, for either he will hate the one and love the other, or he will be devoted to the one and despise the other. You cannot serve God and money.

"Therefore I tell you, do not be anxious about your life, what you will eat or what you will drink, nor about your body, what you will put on. Is not life more than food, and the body more than clothing? Look at the birds of the air: they neither sow nor reap nor gather into barns, and yet your heavenly Father feeds them. Are you not of more value than they? And which of you by being anxious can add a single hour to his span of life? And why are you anxious about clothing? Consider the lilies of the field, how they grow: they neither toil nor spin, yet I tell you, even Solomon in all his glory was not arrayed like one of these. But if God so clothes the grass of the field, which today is alive and tomorrow is thrown into the oven, will he not much more clothe you, O you of little faith? Therefore do not be anxious, saying, 'What shall we eat?' or 'What shall we drink?' or 'What shall we wear?' For the Gentiles seek after all these things, and your heavenly Father knows that you need them all. But seek first the kingdom of God and his righteousness, and all these things will be added to you.

"Therefore do not be anxious about tomorrow, for tomorrow will be anxious for itself. Sufficient for the day is its own trouble."

36 IF JESUS WAS SERIOUS . . . THEN WE LET PEOPLE THINK WHAT THEY WILL ABOUT US.

ONE OF THE MANY graces of growing older is being liberated from what others think about me. I have not been released from this prison fully, but I sense I may be up for parole soon. At the very least, I am more free than my children, who still fear the ridicule of their peers for saying, doing, or wearing the wrong thing. So much of adolescence is pretending to be someone we are not in order to win the approval of other pretenders.

Throughout Matthew 6, Jesus emphasizes the danger of living to win the approval of others rather than of God. He shows how this can infect the authenticity of our giving, praying, and fasting, but these are merely illustrations of the danger. Any element of our life with God can be corrupted when we become more worried about what people think of us than what God thinks of us. The fear of people is a massive barrier to our growth in God's kingdom, and living for the approval of others is a sure way to remain in perpetual spiritual adolescence. In his book *The Divine Conspiracy*, Dallas Willard wrote,

> *If we honestly compared the amount of time in church spent thinking about what others think or might think with the amount of time spent thinking about what God is thinking, we would probably be shocked. . . . Whatever our position in life, if our lives and work are to be of the kingdom of God, we must not have human approval as a primary, or even major, aim. We must lovingly allow people to think whatever they will.*[1]

Create some space for honest reflection and ask yourself, "Whose approval do I desire most?" How might you live differently if you truly did not care what that person thought of you?

 READ MORE **Ezekiel 33:31–32; Proverbs 29:25**

"ALL PEOPLE WILL KNOW YOU ARE MY DISCIPLES BY YOUR _____"

A) BUMPER STICKERS

B) LOVE

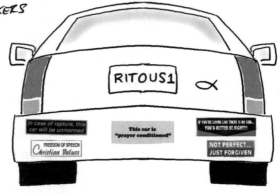

37 IF JESUS WAS SERIOUS . . . THEN WE AVOID DISPLAYS THAT MAKE US APPEAR MORE DEVOUT THAN WE ARE.

IN JESUS' CULTURE, fasting was a mark of deep commitment to God. It was a holy practice for the truly devout. In a society where religiosity was rewarded, to be seen fasting gave a person greater status and prestige. That is why Jesus warned about the dangers of fasting in a way that makes it obvious to others.

Many centuries later, by the time of the Protestant Reformation, the same temptation existed. Martin Luther said fasting had become "a device for having people look at them, talk about them, admire them, and say in astonishment: 'Oh, what wonderful saints these people are! They do not live like the other, ordinary people. They go around in gray coats, with their heads hanging down and sour, pale expressions on their faces. If such people do not get to heaven, what will become of the rest of us?'"[1]

Today, I don't think most people seek approval through flaunting their fasting. In Christian communities, we have different ways of making ourselves appear more righteous than others, and we have new symbols to display our devotion to God. It may be wearing Christian-branded clothing, displaying Jesus junk, or having certain political, cultural, or religious messages on your car's bumper. The particulars vary in different churches and communities, but the temptation to appear better than we are is always present. Consider how you feel this temptation and what you should avoid displaying in order to free yourself from the praise of people.

 READ MORE **Galatians 1:10; 1 Thessalonians 2:3–8**

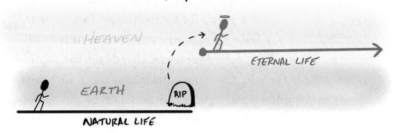

THE POPULAR VIEW

HEAVEN

ETERNAL LIFE

EARTH

RIP

NATURAL LIFE

THE BIBLICAL VIEW

EARTH

HEAVEN

RIP

NATURAL LIFE

ETERNAL LIFE

38 IF JESUS WAS SERIOUS . . . THEN WE WILL DESIRE GOD'S PRESENCE ABOVE ALL ELSE.

WHEN JESUS SAYS, "Do not lay up for yourselves treasures on earth . . . but lay up for yourselves treasures in heaven," we've been conditioned to think of these treasures as future rewards; we assume this is a call to delayed gratification. We assume what Jesus means is: rather than enjoying life now, serve God and His kingdom, and you'll really be well off in the age to come!

This future orientation, however, is not present in Jesus' actual words. There is nothing in this portion of the Sermon on the Mount about a reward awaiting us after death, or about delaying one's gratification until Christ returns. These are ideas we've projected onto the text; they're not in the text itself. Remember, as we discussed earlier, when Jesus speaks about "the heavens," He is talking about a present reality, not a distant realm in the future where the deceased wear robes and play harps.

There are other passages of Scripture that speak of future blessings (like 1 Peter 1:4–5), but Jesus is speaking of something different here. He is talking about a treasure that is accessible to us right now, and this treasure is the presence of God in our lives. We don't have to wait until some future time, or even after our bodily death, to access God's presence and the gifts He possesses. Jesus' point is that having the treasure of God is far more valuable in this life than any treasure the world might offer.

 READ MORE **Hebrews 12:22–24; 1 Peter 1:4–5**

SPIN THE WHEEL OF ULTIMATE CONCERN

"AN IDOL IS USUALLY A GOOD THING THAT WE MAKE ULTIMATE."
—TIM KELLER

WHO'S YOUR GOD?

DEFINE IDENTITY
FIND PURPOSE
PLACE YOUR HOPE

39 IF JESUS WAS SERIOUS . . . THEN WHAT WE TREASURE MOST WILL DEFINE OUR LIVES.

ACCORDING TO theologian Paul Tillich, everyone is religious because everyone has something of ultimate concern. We all have something we treasure above all else. Some will argue that they treasure many things—their children, their spouse, their country, their profession, and maybe God as well. This may be true, but by definition a person can have only one thing of ultimate concern. Whatever this treasure is will define our life and determine our destiny.

For this reason, Jesus tells us to be careful about what we treasure. "No one can serve two masters," He says, and "where your treasure is, there your heart will be also." With these important remarks, Jesus is revealing the power and centrality of our hearts in setting the direction of our lives. As James K. A. Smith explains in his book *You Are What You Love*, we are not primarily thinkers but lovers. We are defined by our affections.

What is your ultimate concern? What occupies your imagination, your daydreaming, and motivates your actions? Jesus warns us to not give the precious, life-defining role of our treasure to anything or anyone unworthy of it—it belongs to God alone.

 READ MORE **Psalm 115:4–8; Mark 12:28–31**

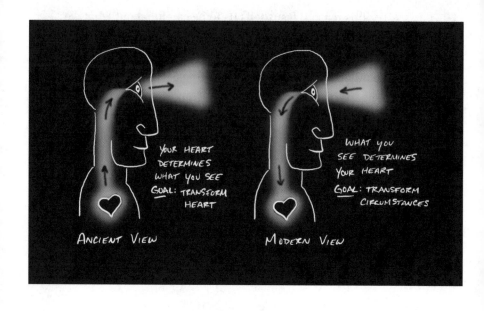

Your heart determines what you see
Goal: Transform heart

What you see determines your heart
Goal: Transform circumstances

ANCIENT VIEW

MODERN VIEW

40

IF JESUS WAS SERIOUS . . . THEN HOW WE SEE THE WORLD WILL BE DETERMINED BY OUR HEART.

AFTER HIS REMARKS about our treasure, and before His warnings about wealth, Jesus speaks about the importance of our eyes. He says, "The eye is the lamp of the body. So, if your eye is healthy, your whole body will be full of light, but if your eye is bad, your whole body will be full of darkness." To modern readers, this business about eyes, light, and darkness sounds both odd and out of place within a discussion of treasure, money, and greed, but to Jesus' ancient audience the connection would have been clear.

Throughout the Sermon on the Mount, Jesus has been focused on our inner orientation because it determines our outward behavior. He does the same here. We know the eye is an organ allowing light to pass into our bodies, making sight possible, but in the ancient world it was thought sight was a process where light passed out of the body through the eyes. Jesus is referencing this common idea to say the way we see the world is an indication of what is inside of us. We either see the world from a righteous perspective (light) or a wicked perspective (darkness).

The words "healthy" and "bad" connect this to the broader economic context. In other passages of Scripture, these words are often translated "generous" and "stingy" or "grudgingly" (see Deut. 15:9 and Matt. 20:15). Jesus is saying the way we handle our wealth is a reflection of what is in our hearts. Those who practice generosity, who see those in need with compassion, are full of light. Those who are greedy, who see only their own need and desire to acquire more for themselves, are full of darkness.

This is more than a call to generosity or warning about greed. To change the way we see the world, Jesus is saying that our inner light—our heart—is what needs transformation.

 READ MORE **Colossians 1:11–13; Deuteronomy 15:7–11**

I THINK YOU'RE IN MY SEAT.

41 IF JESUS WAS SERIOUS . . . THEN WE CANNOT LIVE WITH DIVIDED LOYALTIES.

JESUS TELLS US that we cannot serve more than one master. He was using language familiar to His audience. The relationship between a master and slave was well-established in the first century. While a person could have more than one job, and in some places a husband could have more than one wife, no slave could have more than one master.

Slavery in the United States before the Civil War differed in many ways from the slavery known in the Roman Empire or in ancient Israel, but the expectation of loyalty to one's master remained the same. In Maryland, there was a slave named Jacob who made it his habit to pray three times each day. At regular intervals, he would stop his labor, rest quietly, and commune with God. This enraged his master, a cruel and terrible man named Saunders. While kneeling in the field to pray one day, Saunders approached Jacob and pointed a gun at his head. He ordered him to stop praying and get back to work.

Jacob finished his prayer and then invited Saunders to pull the trigger. "Your loss will be my gain," he said. "I have two masters . . . master Jesus in heaven, and master Saunders on earth. I have a soul and a body; the body belongs to you . . . and the soul to Jesus."[1] Saunders was so shaken by Jacob's lack of fear that he never touched him again. Jacob said he had two masters, but his commitment to prayer—and defiance of Saunders—proved he really had only one.[2]

No one can have more than one master. Who is yours?

 READ MORE **Exodus 20:1–3; Luke 14:25–33**

	$ IDOL OF MONEY	THE LIVING GOD
MAKES ME FEEL SAFE AND SECURE	✓	✓
OFFERS ME POWER OVER THE WORLD	✓	✓
GIVES ME A SENSE OF VALUE & DIGNITY	✓	✓
THERE IS A COMMUNITY THAT SHARES MY WORSHIP	✓	✓
WILL NEVER ABANDON ME EVEN AFTER DEATH		✓

42 IF JESUS WAS SERIOUS . . . THEN WE WILL RECOGNIZE THE ILLUSION OF CONTROL THAT MONEY CREATES.

WHY DOES JESUS single out money as a temptation when there are so many other false masters we may choose to serve other than God?

First, we should note that Jesus is not saying that money or wealth is inherently evil. Scripture is full of godly people with wealth. Some were even disciples of Jesus who funded His ministry. Although it may be used for great good in the hands of a righteous person, money also possesses a dangerous dark side.

Money is an alluring master precisely because it provides the feeling and illusion of divine power. With money, we can control the world and conform it to our will. It allows us to provide for our needs and desires, overcome scarcity, and manipulate those around us. Wealth can isolate us from the challenges that others face; money can create opportunities for those who possess it that are unavailable to those without it. In other words, it is a very appealing alternative to trusting God.

This is why Jesus warned, "It is easier for a camel to go through the eye of a needle than for a rich person to enter the kingdom of God" (Matt. 19:24). A heart dedicated to an idol as powerful as wealth may feel no need to trust in God. In fact, such a heart will seek to reduce God to a tool employed to acquire more money. This is precisely what "prosperity preachers" tell their misguided flocks longing for control over their lives.

The righteous person, however, will do just the opposite. She will surrender control to God and use her wealth as a tool to gain more glory for Him.

 READ MORE **Luke 12:13–21; Hebrews 13:5**

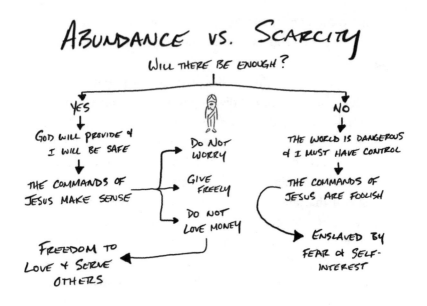

ABUNDANCE VS. SCARCITY

WILL THERE BE ENOUGH?

YES
↓
GOD WILL PROVIDE & I WILL BE SAFE
↓
THE COMMANDS OF JESUS MAKE SENSE

DO NOT WORRY

GIVE FREELY

DO NOT LOVE MONEY

NO
↓
THE WORLD IS DANGEROUS & I MUST HAVE CONTROL
↓
THE COMMANDS OF JESUS ARE FOOLISH
↓
ENSLAVED BY FEAR & SELF-INTEREST

FREEDOM TO LOVE & SERVE OTHERS

43   IF JESUS WAS SERIOUS . . . THEN WE WILL ALWAYS HAVE ENOUGH.

IN 1999, THE RENOWNED Old Testament scholar Walter Brueggemann published an article that greatly influenced me. In it he frames the biblical narrative as a tension between the world's myth of scarcity and God's vision of abundance.

In the Exodus story, for example, Pharaoh and Egypt represent the myth of scarcity. They are threatened by the growth of the Hebrew people, so to protect their power and limited resources, the Egyptians persecuted the Hebrews and killed their children. A fear of scarcity led Pharaoh to violence, injustice, and greed. God's people, on the other hand, experienced His abundance. Every day He provided them with meat and bread in the wilderness, and water miraculously flowed from rocks. Assured of God's provision, they were called to put aside vengeance and greed and instead seek justice, love, kindness, and walk humbly with their God.

In the Sermon on the Mount, Jesus makes the same contrast between the myth of scarcity and the reality of abundance in God's kingdom. If we live in constant fear of not having enough—like Pharaoh did—it will lead us to greed and injustice in the name of self-preservation. If, however, we believe Jesus and trust that with God there is always an abundance, then we can be set free from a self-centered posture and be empowered to truly love others.

How do you see the world? Do you believe in the myth of scarcity, or have you been liberated by the abundance of God's kingdom?

 READ MORE **Exodus 16:1–8; Ephesians 3:20–21**

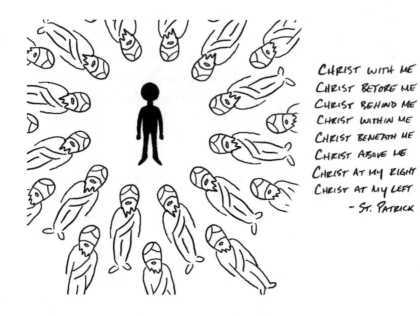

CHRIST WITH ME
CHRIST BEFORE ME
CHRIST BEHIND ME
CHRIST WITHIN ME
CHRIST BENEATH ME
CHRIST ABOVE ME
CHRIST AT MY RIGHT
CHRIST AT MY LEFT
— ST. PATRICK

44 IF JESUS WAS SERIOUS . . . THEN WE WILL NOT BE ENSLAVED BY OUR FEARS.

I LIVE IN CHICAGO, where we commemorate Saint Patrick each year by pouring orange dye into a green river and marveling when it remains green—not exactly a miracle. Amid the shamrocks, leprechauns, and pints of Guinness, few remember the remarkable story of Saint Patrick, but for me he exemplifies Jesus' message in the Sermon on the Mount.

Patrick was not Irish. He was born in Britain, kidnapped as a boy, sold as a slave, and shipped across the sea to Ireland.

While a shepherd in a foreign land, he learned to commune deeply with Christ and trust Him for his needs. His faith grew so strong that years later, after escaping from Ireland, he chose to return to bring the liberating message of Christ to the people who had enslaved him.

Patrick's unwavering faith and lack of fear make him a vivid example of the life without anxiety that Jesus spoke about in the Sermon on the Mount. Rather than worrying about his life, Patrick recognized the presence of his Lord everywhere he went. This prayer, known as the Breastplate of Saint Patrick, captures his vision of the ever-present provision of God. May it inspire you to release your fears as well.

> Christ with me,
> Christ before me,
> Christ behind me,
> Christ in me,
> Christ beneath me,
> Christ above me,
> Christ on my right,
> Christ on my left,
> Christ when I lie down,
> Christ when I sit down,
> Christ when I arise,
> Christ in the heart of every man who thinks of me,
> Christ in the mouth of everyone who speaks of me,
> Christ in every eye that sees me,
> Christ in every ear that hears me.

 READ MORE **Luke 12:32–34; Isaiah 43:1–7**

"FEAR ENGENDERS FEAR. IT NEVER GIVES BIRTH TO LOVE."
— HENRI NOUWEN

45 IF JESUS WAS SERIOUS . . . THEN WE CAN GIVE OURSELVES AWAY FOR THE SAKE OF OTHERS WITHOUT FEAR.

WE HAVE BEEN looking at how the fear of scarcity—not having enough—fills us with anxiety, and Jesus' call in the Sermon on the Mount to surrender this fear by trusting in God's provision. We should not separate this part of Jesus' sermon from His earlier remarks about greed. There is an important connection between fear and generosity.

Thomas Aquinas, the great theologian of the Middle Ages, said fear causes a contraction of the soul. He compared its effect on a person to a city under siege. When an army attacked a city, the inhabitants in the countryside would gather their resources and barricade themselves behind the city's walls. From this contracted, inward-focused position they would hunker down and hope their food and water would outlast the attacking army's will to fight.

Similarly, when we are afraid, we also contract; we pull our resources inward in a posture of protection and self-preservation. We can only think about ourselves, our needs, and our survival. From this defensive position, we cannot love because we cannot give. This is exactly what Jesus wants to set us free from. When we come to see that our heavenly Father will take care of us, we will be released from our captivity to self-centeredness and begin to recognize, and meet, the needs of others. As Henri Nouwen said, "Fear engenders fear. It never gives birth to love."[1]

 READ MORE **Ephesians 4:28; Philippians 2:3–4**

PART 7

JUDGING, ASKING, BLESSING

"Judge not, that you be not judged. For with the judgment you pronounce you will be judged, and with the measure you use it will be measured to you. Why do you see the speck that is in your brother's eye, but do not notice the log that is in your own eye? Or how can you say to your brother, 'Let me take the speck out of your eye,' when there is the log in your own eye? You hypocrite, first take the log out of your own eye, and then you will see clearly to take the speck out of your brother's eye.

"Do not give dogs what is holy, and do not throw your pearls before pigs, lest they trample them underfoot and turn to attack you.

"Ask, and it will be given to you; seek, and you will find; knock, and it will be opened to you. For everyone who asks receives, and the one who seeks finds, and to the one who knocks it will be opened. Or which one of you, if his son asks him for bread, will give him a stone? Or if he asks for a fish, will give him a serpent? If you then, who are evil, know how to give good gifts to your children, how much more will your Father who is in heaven give good things to those who ask him!

"So whatever you wish that others would do to you, do also to them, for this is the Law and the Prophets."

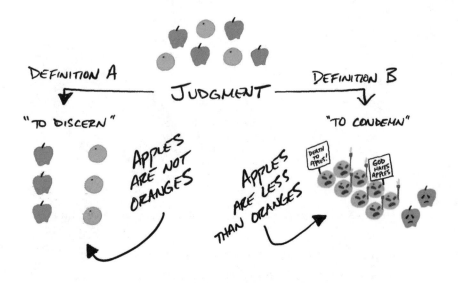

46 IF JESUS WAS SERIOUS . . . THEN WE WILL SEE THE DIFFERENCE BETWEEN DISCERNMENT AND JUDGMENT.

JESUS TOLD HIS disciples, "Judge not, that you be not judged." This is perhaps one of the most frequently quoted verses in Scripture, and it is a favorite even among nonbelievers. It appears to fit the accommodating spirit of our age that sees all choices as valid and all values as equally noble.

The popularity of this verse, I suspect, arises from a

misunderstanding of its meaning. The Greek word "judge" in the New Testament has two meanings, just as it does in English. It can mean discerning between things, as in "I judged the red car to be in better condition than the blue one." If Jesus meant for us to avoid acts of discernment, it would render all of His teachings, not to mention all of Scripture, meaningless. Let's remember that in the same sermon where He says, "judge not" He also calls us to discern between right and wrong, good and evil (Matt. 7:15–20).

The second meaning of "judge" is to sit in a place of superiority to condemn. This is the sort of judgment Jesus warns against. He does not want us to condemn others, to pass final judgment upon them, or declare another person to be irretrievably guilty. Such devaluing of a person is precisely what Jesus' enemies did to Him—it is the way of the world, not the way of God's kingdom.

 READ MORE **Exodus 20:13; 1 Corinthians 4:5**

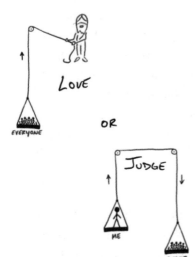

"YOU CAN'T LOVE & JUDGE AT THE SAME TIME. IT'S IMPOSSIBLE TO ASCRIBE UNSURPASSABLE WORTH TO OTHERS WHEN YOU'RE USING OTHERS TO ASCRIBE WORTH TO YOURSELF."
—GREG BOYD

47 IF JESUS WAS SERIOUS . . . THEN WE CANNOT JUDGE AND LOVE AT THE SAME TIME.

THE KIND OF judgment Jesus forbids is the sort that condemns another person. Sinful judgment devalues a person or group of people. It diminishes their inherent worth as those made in God's image. Instead, they become seen as a sub-human species undeserving of our respect or love. In some cases, the judgment may cause us to think they are unworthy of life itself. The command to "judge not" is a warning not to exclude anyone from the reach of God's love or to see ourselves or our group as inherently superior to another.

We may disagree with our neighbors, and we may discern another person or group to be wrong, but when this discernment leads us to value our neighbor less, that is when we cross from discernment into judgment, condemnation, and ungodly exclusion. Sadly, this sort of rhetoric fills our culture today and has been applauded by many. It has become acceptable, even among some Christians, to condemn those who hold different religious, cultural, or political beliefs. We are quick to call them enemies and reluctant to love them as neighbors.

When we condemn another, we are declaring they have no worth—they do not matter to us or God. This impulse to judge is often a way of elevating ourselves by devaluing another. One pastor puts it this way: "You can't love and judge at the same time," because "It's impossible to ascribe unsurpassable worth to others when you're using others to ascribe worth to yourself."[1]

 READ MORE **Matthew 15:1–14; Hebrews 5:12–14**

48 IF JESUS WAS SERIOUS . . . THEN WE WILL PRACTICE SELF-AWARENESS AND NOT SELF-RIGHTEOUSNESS.

WHY IS IT SO EASY to see others' faults and so difficult to see our own? Jesus tells us to remove the plank in our own eye before we seek to remove the speck in our brother's. It is a call to self-awareness rather than self-righteousness. We see vivid examples of this in the story of Jesus' own arrest and suffering.

Consider the duplicity of the Sanhedrin. They could have

arrested Jesus while He taught openly at the temple. Instead, they snatched Him in the middle of the night outside the city to avoid public outcry. Then they held a trial under the cover of darkness so no one could come to Jesus' defense. Finally, the Sanhedrin arranged for false witnesses to testify against Jesus to fabricate a reason to execute Him. They used their power to protect their status rather than seek justice. They manipulated the judicial system against an innocent man in order to maintain control.

The Sanhedrin repeatedly, blatantly broke God's law, all the while they were attempting to find just one speck of sin in Jesus' eye. They were so blinded by their self-righteousness that they could no longer discern right from wrong or godliness from wickedness.

This is a warning to all of us who cling to a religious identity while judging the nonreligious people around us. We may become so convinced of our righteousness that we fail to see our own duplicity. When you feel the impulse to judge another, instead consider praying, "Lord, show me the plank in my own eye."

 READ MORE **Mark 14:55–56; 1 Corinthians 4:5**

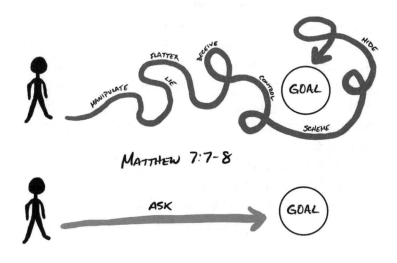

MATTHEW 7:7-8

49 IF JESUS WAS SERIOUS . . . THEN WE WILL ASK, RATHER THAN MANIPULATE, OTHERS FOR WHAT WE NEED.

WHEN JESUS SAYS, "Ask, and it will be given to you; seek, and you will find; knock, and it will be opened to you," we automatically think he is speaking about prayer and our relationship with God. That is appropriate because Jesus applies this to prayer in the verses that follow. Rather than attempting to twist or manipulate God into blessing us, Jesus invites us to trust His goodness by simply asking Him for what we need. But we must not dismiss what has come before this statement in the sermon either.

Before the famous ask-seek-knock passage, Jesus spoke about judging others and the hypocrisy of focusing on our brother's failure rather than our own. The invitation to ask-seek-knock comes first within the context of how we relate to our brothers and sisters, and only after that is it applied to how we relate to our heavenly Father.[1]

Jesus appears to be juxtaposing two ways of motivating people to do what we desire. The world's way is through judgment and force. It happens by elevating one's self and demeaning others—by exposing their faults and hiding one's own. In other words, we try to control people through manipulation and deceit. The alternative method, and the one appropriate for life in God's kingdom, is simple: just ask.

Asking others for what we need or want is difficult for two reasons. First, it requires being honest and vulnerable about our intention. We must risk exposing ourselves to the rejection of others. Second, asking is difficult because it affirms the dignity and status of the other person as our equal—or our superior. In other words, asking requires humility. If we learn to ask for what we need with honesty and humility rather than scheming for it, Jesus says we will discover a far better way of life with both God and others.

 READ MORE **James 4:2–3; Nehemiah 2:1–6**

50   IF JESUS WAS SERIOUS . . . THEN GOD ALREADY WANTS TO BLESS US; HE DOESN'T NEED CONVINCING.

JESUS COMPARES our heavenly Father's disposition toward us with the kindness of our earthly fathers. What father would give his child a stone when he asks for bread, Jesus asks, or a serpent when they ask for a fish? The love of even the very best father is imperfect, but they still know how to give good gifts to their children. Our heavenly Father's love is without limit or shadow, Jesus said, so how much more will He give good things to us when we ask Him?

Within this teaching, Jesus is rejecting two very common ideas held by many religious people. First, He is rejecting the popular vision of a capricious, malevolent god. Jesus teaches that God is not a God who begrudgingly blesses His people, but instead a loving Father who wants to bless us. We are not slaves in God's household, hoping He will take notice of us and offer us a scrap from His table. We are sons and daughters who are invited to His table to share in the abundance of His wealth.

Second, Jesus is rejecting the common belief that blessings must be manipulated or coerced from God through rituals or demonstrations of piety. Very often, religious people assume God's goodness will be available to them only if they attend church more regularly, give more sacrificially, or pray more earnestly. Rather than seeing God as a loving Father, they engage Him as if He were an unstable child who must be bribed into obedience. Not only does this view violate the clear evidence of God's kindness, it also sinfully assumes we possess the power to manipulate Him like a puppet on a string.

A correct vision of God and ourselves should lead to a completely different way of engagement. That is why Jesus invites us to simply ask Him. Unlike other religious traditions, Jesus bestows on us the dignity of children rather than the humiliation of slaves.

 READ MORE **2 Chronicles 1:7–12; Philippians 4:6–7**

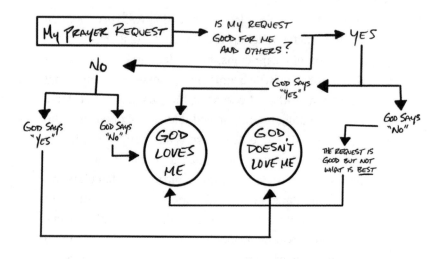

IF JESUS WAS SERIOUS . . .
THEN WHEN GOD SAYS NO, IT'S
BECAUSE HE LOVES US TOO MUCH
TO SAY YES.

JESUS SAYS GOD hears our prayers with the ears of a loving
Father who gives good things to His children. With this image
of God in mind, we are to ask for what we desire. This has led
some to think incorrectly that God will grant whatever we ask.
No parent always says yes to their child. Sometimes saying no is
proof of a parent's love, not its absence.

On a trip to New Delhi with my father many years ago, we were approached by a young boy on the street. He was rail thin, virtually naked, and his legs were stiff and contorted like a wire hanger twisted on itself. He waddled on his hands and kneecaps over the broken pavement. The boy hounded us with his shouts. "One rupee, please! One rupee!" Finally, my father stopped.

"What do you want?" he asked.

"One rupee, sir," the boy said. My father laughed.

"How about I give you five rupees?" he said. The boy's countenance suddenly became defiant. He retracted his hand and sneered at us. He thought my father was joking, having a laugh at his expense. After all, no one would give five rupees when he asked for only one. The boy started shuffling away, mumbling curses under his breath. When he heard the jingle of the coins, however, the boy stopped and looked back over his shoulder. My father was holding out a five-rupee coin and placed it in the boy's hand. Stunned, he didn't move or say a word.

This, I imagine, is how our God sees us: miserable creatures in desperate need of His help. Rather than asking for what we truly need, rather than desiring what He is able and willing to give, we settle for lesser things. And when God graciously says no to our misled requests and instead offers us more, we reject Him. We turn away, cursing Him under our breath.

When our Lord says no to our desires, it is because He loves us too much to say yes. He wants to offer us something far more valuable. He offers us Himself.[1]

 READ MORE **2 Corinthians 12:8–10; Hebrews 12:5–11**

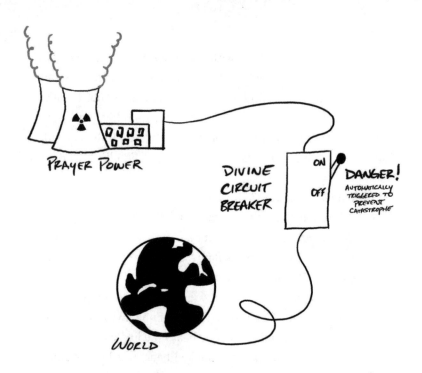

PRAYER POWER

DIVINE
CIRCUIT
BREAKER

ON
OFF

DANGER!
AUTOMATICALLY
TRIGGERED TO
PREVENT
CATASTROPHE

WORLD

52   IF JESUS WAS SERIOUS . . . THEN PRAYER IS FAR MORE POWERFUL THAN WE THINK.

JESUS' INVITATION to simply ask our heavenly Father for what we need is a radical departure from what most religions—both ancient and modern—prescribe. Most often, we are taught that God's favor must be won with gifts, rituals, sacrifices, or obedience before considering something as bold as a direct request of the divine. Religion usually puts us in the role of slaves in God's world, but Jesus exalts us to the status of children in God's home.

The great power and dignity granted to us, however, does not mean all we seek from God will be given to us. Some view unanswered requests as a sign of prayer's weakness, but C. S. Lewis said just the opposite. It is precisely because prayer is so powerful that our use of it must be confined. In his essay "Work and Prayer," he wrote,

> *Prayers are not always . . . "granted." This is not because prayer is a weaker kind of causality, but because it is a stronger kind. When it "works" at all it works unlimited by space and time. That is why God has retained a discretionary power of granting or refusing it; except on that condition prayer would destroy us.*[1]

If Lewis is correct, and I think he is, far from being disappointed, we ought to be grateful when a desire expressed in prayer is not granted. Such a posture will seem absurd, but only to those who have not yet been convinced of God's complete and utter goodness toward His children.

 READ MORE **Galatians 4:6–7; James 5:14–16**

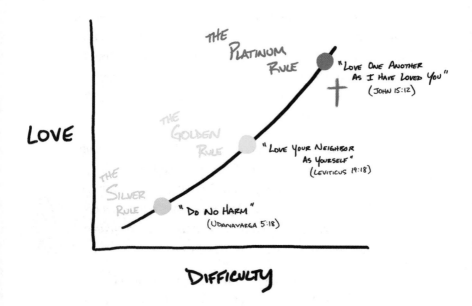

LOVE

THE PLATINUM RULE

THE GOLDEN RULE

THE SILVER RULE

"LOVE ONE ANOTHER AS I HAVE LOVED YOU" (JOHN 15:12)

"LOVE YOUR NEIGHBOR AS YOURSELF" (LEVITICUS 19:18)

"DO NO HARM" (UDANAVARGA 5:18)

DIFFICULTY

53 IF JESUS WAS SERIOUS . . . THEN MERELY TOLERATING THOSE WHO ARE DIFFERENT ISN'T ENOUGH.

MOHANDAS GANDHI once wrote, "Religions are different roads converging to the same point. What does it matter that we take different roads, so long as we reach the same goal?"[1] His sentiment has become very popular in our globalized, relativistic culture, and it is often linked to platitudes about the

Golden Rule being at the heart of all religions. However comforting this idea may be, it remains entirely untrue.

Eastern religions like Jainism, Buddhism, and Hinduism are predicated on the rule of Ahimsa, which means to "do no harm" or "cause no injury" to any living creature. This is certainly an admirable calling, but as popularly practiced fails to capture the fullness of what Jesus taught with His Golden Rule. For this reason, some have called Ahimsa the Silver Rule—it is good but there is something better.

In the Sermon on the Mount, Jesus commanded, "Whatever you wish that others would do to you, do also to them." This is more than a call to avoid harm or injury; it is a command to active love. As Dallas Willard notes, "The Golden Rule is devoted to the good in the lives of those around us, and this reaches far beyond the mere absence of harm . . . it aspires toward a remarkable richness in their lives, not simply the alleviation of their suffering."[2]

Some religions should be commended for leading us on a path of nonviolence and a "live-and-let-live" tolerance. The path of Christ, however, leads us to far more. It seeks the flourishing of all through self-sacrificial love.

 READ MORE **Romans 13:8–10; John 15:12–13**

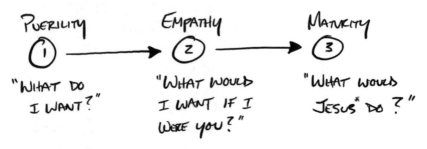

MORAL DEVELOPMENT

PUERILITY	EMPATHY	MATURITY
① ⟶	② ⟶	③
"WHAT DO I WANT?"	"WHAT WOULD I WANT IF I WERE YOU?"	"WHAT WOULD JESUS* DO?"

* KNOWLEDGE ABOUT JESUS NOT INCLUDED. SOME SPIRITUAL FORMATION REQUIRED.

54 IF JESUS WAS SERIOUS . . . THEN OUR CONSCIENCE, NOT JUST OUR BELIEFS, WILL GUIDE HOW WE TREAT OTHERS.

IN THE 1990s, "What Would Jesus Do?" merchandise became very popular. Millions of T-shirts, bracelets, and baubles were marked with W.W.J.D. to remind us to behave like Jesus. Yet this admirable call suffers from one significant shortcoming. To answer the question "What would Jesus do?" a person must possess enough knowledge about Jesus to extrapolate what He would do in any given circumstance. If research is to be believed, this is knowledge that most Americans—including those who call themselves Christians—do not possess.[1]

Thankfully, in the Sermon on the Mount we are provided a more accessible moral imperative. The Golden Rule is predicated on self-knowledge rather than divine knowledge. When determining how to respond to others, rather than asking W.W.J.D.? The Golden Rule instructs us to ask W.W.I.W.—"What would I want?" Rather than setting the bar inaccessibly high by saying we should act like Jesus, the Golden Rule puts obedience within our reach by making our own conscience the standard. In any given circumstance we are to treat others the way we want to be treated.

The enduring brilliance of the Golden Rule is found in its universality. It can be followed by anyone, anytime, in any culture as long as the person is self-aware enough to acknowledge her own desires. Begin your time of prayer today by selecting one or two difficult people in your life. Ask yourself, "If I were _____, what would I want today?" Commit to treating these people as you would want to be treated.

 READ MORE **Matthew 22:34–40; Galatians 5:14**

PART 8

GOOD AND BAD FRUIT

"Enter by the narrow gate. For the gate is wide and the way is easy that leads to destruction, and those who enter by it are many. For the gate is narrow and the way is hard that leads to life, and those who find it are few.

"Beware of false prophets, who come to you in sheep's clothing but inwardly are ravenous wolves. [16]You will recognize them by their fruits. Are grapes gathered from thorn bushes, or figs from thistles? So, every healthy tree bears good fruit, but the diseased tree bears bad fruit. A healthy tree cannot bear bad fruit, nor can a diseased tree bear good fruit. Every tree that does not bear good fruit is cut down and thrown into the fire. Thus you will recognize them by their fruits.

"Not everyone who says to me, 'Lord, Lord,' will enter the kingdom of heaven, but the one who does the will of my Father who is in heaven. On that day many will say to me, 'Lord, Lord, did we not prophesy in your name, and cast out demons in your name, and do many mighty works in your name?' And then will I declare to them, 'I never knew you; depart from me, you workers of lawlessness.'"

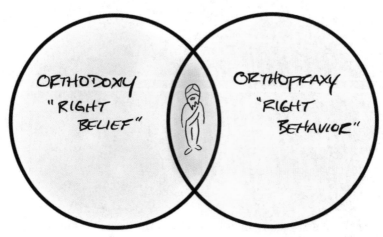

ORTHODOXY − ORTHOPRAXY = HYPOCRISY

ORTHODOXY + ORTHOPRAXY = CHRISTIANITY

55   IF JESUS WAS SERIOUS . . . THEN HE ACTUALLY EXPECTS US TO DO WHAT HE SAID.

JESUS' SERMON in Matthew 5–7 was not the first one delivered from a mountain to God's people. In the Old Testament, Moses pronounced God's commandments and covenant with Israel from Mount Sinai. At the conclusion of that defining sermon, God called His people to obedience. "When Moses went and told the people all the LORD's words and laws, they responded with one voice, 'Everything the LORD has said we will do'" (Ex. 24:3 NIV).

This is a frequent theme in Scripture. After hearing God's commands, His people are given a choice. They may follow the ways of other nations and gods, which leads only to destruction, or they can choose to follow the Lord on the path to life and flourishing. Jesus employs this same pattern in His Sermon on the Mount.

Having described the way of His kingdom, Jesus concludes His teaching with multiple calls to obedience first with the imagery of paths and gates (Matt. 7:13–14), then with a warning about those who appear obedient but are not (7:15–23), and finishes with a parable about foolish and wise builders (7:24–27). Jesus' triple conclusion to His sermon is intended to emphasize one message: just do it.

Jesus did not intend His sermon to be a beautiful ethical theory or a righteous but unattainable ideal. The evidence is overwhelming that He expects us to do what He taught. Just as the Israelites responded to Moses, we are to respond to Jesus by declaring, "Everything the Lord has said we will do."

 READ MORE **James 1:22–25; Psalm 1:1–6**

56 IF JESUS WAS SERIOUS . . . THEN WE WILL BE SUSPICIOUS OF POPULARITY.

DESPITE THEIR OVERUSE, advertisers know that super-latives sell. Every business wants its product to be the "most prescribed," "most trusted," "most watched," or "bestselling." These phrases all communicate the same thing to the buyer: millions of people can't be wrong. This message comforts the consumer because we feel like part of the crowd when we purchase a popular product. It feeds into our broken, insecure human nature that longs for acceptance. In a consumer culture, a product's perceived value is directly proportional to the number of people it impacts. Popularity not only means success; it also means legitimacy.[1]

This is why Jesus' dismissal of popularity in the Sermon on the Mount can confuse and even offend us. He warned that the popular path with the wide gate leads only to destruction, "and those who enter by it are many." Instead, He calls His followers to the unpopular, narrow way that is difficult and traveled by few. Clearly, Jesus is unschooled in successful marketing techniques. Perhaps because He was more focused on faithfulness than on effectiveness (at least as the world defines it).

Those of us formed by a consumer culture and shaped by a tradition of Christianity that strives for popularity and broad acceptance need to wrestle with Jesus' words. In our desire to make Jesus appealing, are we tempted to abandon the narrow path? Are we presenting to people the God who really is, or merely the god they want? And in your own Christian life, are you following leaders or ideas merely because they are popular, or are you discerning their conformity to Jesus and His way? Beware the pitfalls of popularity.

 READ MORE **John 6:60–69; Isaiah 53:1–3**

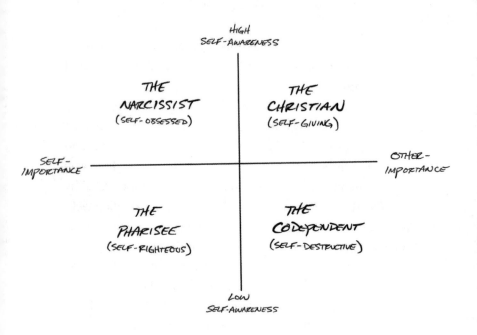

HIGH
SELF-AWARENESS

THE NARCISSIST
(SELF-OBSESSED)

THE CHRISTIAN
(SELF-GIVING)

SELF-IMPORTANCE

OTHER-IMPORTANCE

THE PHARISEE
(SELF-RIGHTEOUS)

THE CODEPENDENT
(SELF-DESTRUCTIVE)

LOW
SELF-AWARENESS

57 IF JESUS WAS SERIOUS . . . THEN THE NARROW WAY WILL NEVER BE A LONELY WAY.

JESUS' CALL TO take the unpopular, narrow road should not be misunderstood as a call to isolation or spiritual privacy. In our hyperindividualistic culture, and as public forms of Christianity fall out of favor, it may be assumed that the way of Jesus can be properly followed only by recluses and monks. This is entirely false. The narrow path is not the lonely path.

The call of Jesus is always a call into community. He collected disciples from disparate parts of His culture—fishermen

148

and Pharisees, tax collectors and political dissidents—and formed them into a community. He instructed them not to go into the villages alone but sent them in pairs. Scripture calls us to love, encourage, and serve one another. It is when we walk the narrow road together, Jesus taught, that He would be in our midst.

That may be the most comforting reminder of all. We do not take the narrow way because it is easy, or because we long to be different. We do not take it merely because the wide road leads to destruction. We take it because on it we encounter the presence of Jesus. Dietrich Bonhoeffer said it this way:

> As long as I recognize this road as the one I am commanded to walk, and try to walk it in fear of myself, it is truly impossible. But if I see Jesus Christ walking ahead of me, step by step, if I look only at him and follow him, step by step, then I will be protected on this path.[1]

 READ MORE **Hebrews 10:24–25; Luke 24:13–32**

WHICH FRUIT DO YOU LOOK FOR?

THE EVANGELICAL INDUSTRIAL COMPLEX	THE KINGDOM OF GOD
• EFFECTIVENESS	• GENEROSITY
• POWER	• MERCY
• IMPACT	• HONESTY
• INFLUENCE	• GENTLENESS
• POPULARITY	• FAITHFULNESS
• RELEVANCE	• HUMILITY

58 IF JESUS WAS SERIOUS . . . THEN OUR CHARACTER MATTERS MORE THAN OUR ACCOMPLISHMENTS.

YEARS AGO, I interviewed a successful pastor nearing retirement. Early in his ministry, his church grew rapidly. Thousands flocked to hear him every weekend, other pastors sought his advice on how to grow their churches, and he even received awards for the effectiveness of his ministry. From the outside, everything looked wonderful and blessed by God.

The pastor told me, however, that his inner life was an ugly mess and the people closest to him saw it. His marriage was near collapse, his children resented him, and his communion with God was almost nonexistent. His soul was producing anger, bitterness, and anxiety.

In the Sermon on the Mount, Jesus said we will recognize people by what they produce: "A healthy tree cannot bear bad fruit, nor can a diseased tree bear good fruit." The problem illustrated by the pastor I interviewed is that we often look at the wrong fruit; we are culturally conditioned to assess people—including ministry leaders—by their professional success. How effective is he? How many people have been impacted? How much has she achieved? We incorrectly assume that an effective leader (as defined by our culture) must be a godly leader.

In the context of the Sermon on the Mount, it is clear that the "fruit" Jesus is looking for is defined by character, not accomplishments. Throughout the sermon, He focuses on inner qualities such as anger, love, lust, generosity, hypocrisy, honesty, anxiety, and peace. This means it is entirely possible to be a celebrated leader with an huge ministry and be a diseased tree producing rotten fruit. It also means that healthy trees with godly fruit may not achieve measurable success that the world will praise.

 READ MORE **Galatians 5:22; Psalm 1:1–6**

ABIDE OR ASSEMBLE?

HOW FRUIT HAPPENS
(JOHN 15:1-5)

FRUIT MANUFACTURING CO.

HOW THE EVANGELICAL
INDUSTRIAL COMPLEX
THINKS FRUIT HAPPENS

59 IF JESUS WAS SERIOUS . . . THEN WE WILL PRODUCE GOOD FRUIT NATURALLY AND EFFORTLESSLY.

WE LIVE IN A self-improvement culture. We believe that whatever is undesirable, deficient, or undeveloped in us can be changed with a combination of knowledge and willpower. I just need to read the right book, get into the right program, or work the right system to become the person I want to be.

Yet Jesus presents a different vision of human potential. He compares people to trees. The fruit a tree produces, He said, is determined by the identity of the tree. A good tree will produce good fruit; a bad tree will produce bad fruit. An apple tree cannot produce apricots, and a peach tree cannot make kumquats. No amount of knowledge, willpower, or effort will change what a tree produces; it is inherent to the tree's identity. Fruit just happens.

This is perplexing to Christians in our self-improvement culture. When we read that the fruit of the Spirit "is love, joy, peace, patience, kindness, goodness, faithfulness, gentleness, self-control," we immediately look for the program that will produce more of these qualities in our lives. We assume that patience is improved by directly pursuing more patience. The call of Christ, however, is not to improve our fruit but to instead seek the transformation of our identity. Our old selves must be uprooted and a new self planted in God. We must become trees rooted in God and thriving on His Spirit. Then we will naturally—even effortlessly—produce His good fruit.

 READ MORE **Matthew 11:25–30; Galatians 5:16–25**

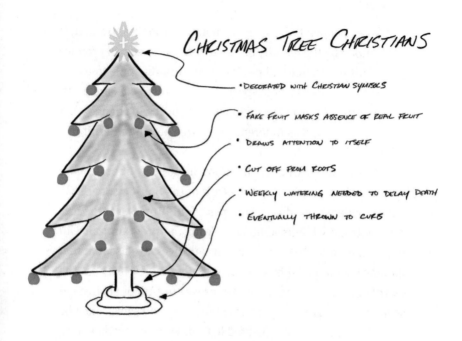

CHRISTMAS TREE CHRISTIANS

- Decorated with Christian symbols
- Fake fruit masks absence of real fruit
- Draws attention to itself
- Cut off from roots
- Weekly watering needed to delay death
- Eventually thrown to curb

60 IF JESUS WAS SERIOUS . . . THEN WE WILL FOCUS MORE ON OUR LIFE WITH GOD RATHER THAN OUR WORK FOR HIM.

A GOOD TREE will naturally and automatically produce good fruit. That is how Jesus described His disciples. We are like healthy, thriving trees and the life of God within us is manifested in the love, joy, peace, kindness, and mercy we produce. The key to this kind of life, Jesus said, is learning to abide deeply in communion with Him the way a branch abides in a vine or a tree that is rooted in good soil. Our focus should not be the fruit on our branches but the depth of our roots. As we live deeply with Jesus, the fruit will take care of itself.

In many Christian communities, however, there are great social pressures to appear godly. This tempts us to focus almost exclusively upon visible, easily measurable fruitfulness—which often gets confused with effectiveness. Rather than developing a life rooted in Christ through prayer, we worry more about displaying the right behaviors and symbols in front of others. When we do this we become Christmas tree Christians.

Christmas trees are beautiful and they draw attention to themselves in a way natural trees do not. They are decorated with tinsel and lights and covered with glittering glass fruit, but all of the ornaments are there to hide the unappealing truth—Christmas trees are corpses. They are dead, cut off from their roots, and sustained by a pot of water that must be refilled—perhaps every Sunday morning. Eventually every Christmas tree has its fake fruit removed and it is thrown to the curb or burned.

Too many of our communities are filled with beautiful but dead Christmas trees, yet what our Lord desires is the subtle beauty of a fruitful, thriving orchard.

 READ MORE **Matthew 23:25–28; John 15:1–6**

61 IF JESUS WAS SERIOUS . . . THEN KNOWING A LEADER'S QUALITY REQUIRES TIME AND PROXIMITY.

FALSE LEADERS are difficult to identify in the church, which is why Jesus compares them to wolves in sheep's clothing. Externally they appear righteous, godly, and sufficiently "Christian." They use the right words, express the right ideas, and may even display the right symbols and activities. However, in the Sermon on the Mount, Jesus warns that if we only look at the surface we will be easily deceived by false prophets.

Instead, we are called to identify a person by what is beneath the surface, past the clothing and religious disguises. But how? We need spiritual X-ray vision. Unlike Superman's ability to see through disguises instantly, spiritual X-ray vision requires two things: time and proximity. Jesus said that a person's true identity, like a tree, is revealed by their "fruit." We cannot know a tree's identity from a mile away. We must get close to it, and we won't know the tree's quality until the seasons have passed. Properly identifying a tree's fruit and quality requires time and proximity.

The same goes for leaders. Sadly, these two qualities are undervalued in too many churches today. We are content granting enormous spiritual authority to people we encounter only on screens at a great distance, and the temptation of trends means we rarely stay anywhere long enough to see the real fruit of a leader's life. Brief, distant engagement with leaders is the perfect scenario for wolves to flourish. We should not be surprised to find churches and ministries devoured when the importance of proximity to, and time with, leaders is dismissed. If you want to know the true identity of those influencing your faith, if you want to have spiritual X-ray vision, pursue time and proximity with your leaders.

 READ MORE **1 Samuel 16:7; Jeremiah 23:1–6**

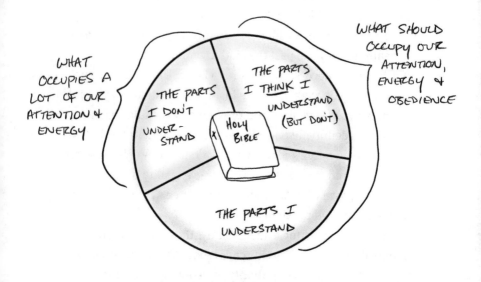

WHAT OCCUPIES A LOT OF OUR ATTENTION & ENERGY

THE PARTS I DON'T UNDERSTAND

THE PARTS I THINK I UNDERSTAND (BUT DON'T)

HOLY BIBLE

WHAT SHOULD OCCUPY OUR ATTENTION, ENERGY & OBEDIENCE

THE PARTS I UNDERSTAND

62 | IF JESUS WAS SERIOUS . . . THEN MANY WILL BE SURPRISED ON THE DAY OF JUDGMENT.

MARK TWAIN IS reported to have said, "It ain't those parts of the Bible that I can't understand that bother me, it's the parts that I do understand."[1] Matthew 7:21–23 is one of those parts of the Bible for me. I've studied it, I've come to an understanding of it, and it bothers me because it deconstructs so many of the assumptions we hold.

This passage fits within the series of warnings Jesus gives at the end of the Sermon on the Mount. He warns His disciples to choose the narrow way that leads to life rather than the popular way that leads to destruction (7:13–14). Then He warns them about false prophets, the wolves in sheep's clothing who appear godly but are in fact opposed to God's kingdom (7:15–20). In His next warning, Jesus continues His explanation of false prophets, but embedded in His remarks is a call to self-examination for everyone who claims to belong to Christ.

Jesus speaks of the day of judgment and the danger of delusion. There will be people, He says, who will plead their case before Him. They will claim to belong to Christ because of the power and magnitude of their words and works. But He will dismiss them with the horrible truth, "I never knew you." For me, this is the most frightening passage in all of Scripture, and in pages ahead I will explain why. But for now, let me draw your attention to the most frightening word in this passage: "many." Jesus says "many" will be convinced that they belong to God and be horrified when they are cast away from His presence.

I encourage you to read and reflect on this text, and then ask yourself: *Why do I think I belong to Christ? Where have I put my confidence?*

 READ MORE **Hosea 8:1–8; Luke 6:46**

63 IF JESUS WAS SERIOUS . . . THEN CALLING HIM "LORD" ISN'T ENOUGH.

MY WIFE AND I were friends in high school. One day she called and enthusiastically announced that her dad had just bought her a car.

"What kind?" I asked.

"It's a Ferrari!" she declared.

"Your dad did not buy you a Ferrari," I replied.

"Yes he did," she insisted. I needed proof.

"Drive it over and let me see it," I said.

What pulled into my driveway was a fifteen-year-old rusty, vomit-colored Firebird with a broken suspension and no exhaust system. Amanda kept calling it a Ferrari for weeks, but nothing she said could change the fact that her jalopy was not an exotic Italian sports car.

Sometimes we deceive ourselves with words or buy into the magical thinking that saying something enough makes it true. In His discourse about the final judgment, Jesus warned against this error. He said, "Not everyone who says to me, 'Lord, Lord,' will enter the kingdom of heaven, but the one who does the will of my Father who is in heaven."

We may say that Jesus is our Lord, but that alone does not make it so. The true lord of our life is revealed by our actions not by our declarations. If we are to enter Jesus' kingdom, He must actually be our King, and if we persistently live in a manner that denies His authority, no amount of verbal praise and exaltation will make Him so.

 READ MORE **James 1:22; Matthew 21:28–32**

How to Fail the Final Judgment

- [A+] Right Theology
- [A+] Bold Preaching
- [A+] Fights Evil/Injustice
- [A+] Performs Miracles
- [F] Communion w/God

MATT 7:21-23

FAIL

64 IF JESUS WAS SERIOUS . . . THEN GOOD THEOLOGY AND SPECTACULAR MINISTRY ISN'T ENOUGH.

WE'VE ALREADY looked at the danger of words without actions. Those who call Jesus "Lord" but do not act like it are deluding themselves. We might conclude from Jesus' warning that a life full of godly activity in His name is what He is looking for, but that would be a hasty and foolish conclusion as well.

Jesus goes on to say, "Many will say to me on that day, 'Lord, Lord, did we not prophesy in your name and in your name drive out demons and in your name perform many miracles?' Then I will tell them plainly, 'I never knew you. Away from me, you evildoers!" (Matt. 7:22 NIV).

The people Jesus describes in this section of the Sermon on the Mount are full of words and spectacular actions. These are people who appear to be zealous for Christ and His mission; they call Him, "Lord, Lord," which is more than a title of respect. In the context of the final judgment it is an affirmation of His divinity. They believe Jesus has the authority to judge on the last day—a role Jews believed belonged to God alone. In other words, the people Jesus addresses here believe He is God.

They also prophesy. This means they proclaim God's words—they are ministry leaders and preachers. Finally, they are full of power—they cast out demons and perform miracles. And they do all of this in Jesus' name. The people Jesus describes appear to be very impressive. They are the kind of Christian leaders that we celebrate and elevate.

How could such people—leaders full of power with effective ministries and dynamic preaching, who affirm Jesus' deity—be excluded from His kingdom? Why would Jesus ever say to such people, "Away from me"?

We'll address that question soon, but for now ask yourself, what impresses you? What qualities do you look for in a Christian leader, and what has shaped your view? Is it possible that what impresses you may not impress Jesus?

 READ MORE **Isaiah 1:11–17; 2 Timothy 4:3–4**

WHAT IMPRESSES US

WHAT PLEASES GOD

THE SPECTACULAR
WORLD-CHANGER

THE INVISIBLE
MERCY-GIVER

65   IF JESUS WAS SERIOUS . . . THEN LOVE REALLY IS WHAT MATTERS MOST.

THE KEY TO understanding the judgment scene in the Sermon on the Mount is found in the word "evildoers." Jesus says, "Away from me, you evildoers!" (Matt. 7:23 NIV). The word "evildoers" may be more literally translated "those who practice lawlessness." Jesus is saying these people did not submit to His authority. They never really surrendered themselves to God. While these false Christians were full of God's works—preaching, exorcisms, miracles—they were not obedient to God's will. They never released control.

This fits with Jesus' previous declaration that He "never knew" them. Despite their abundance of works in Jesus' name, they had no relationship with Him. There was no intimacy—no genuine knowledge of, or submission to, His will.

We may see a link between the "evildoers" in this text and what Jesus says about "lawlessness," which is the same word, later in Matthew 24:12. There He links it with false prophets causing love to grow cold. Taken together, we begin to see a picture of Christians who claim God's name and perform mighty works but ignore the most important aspect of God's will—to love Him and others. Throughout the Bible, God's will is identified far more often with acts of compassion, mercy, and love than with impressive displays of power. False Christianity always inverts this by preferring spectacular works over humble obedience and sacrificial love.

 READ MORE **1 Corinthians 13:1–3; Matthew 24:41–46**

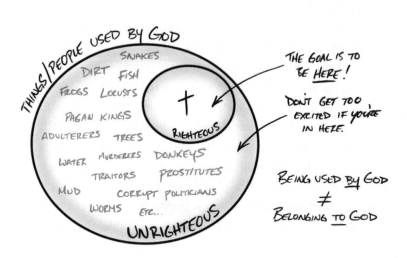

THINGS/PEOPLE USED BY GOD

SNAKES
DIRT FISH
FROGS LOCUSTS
PAGAN KINGS
ADULTERERS TREES RIGHTEOUS
WATER MURDERERS DONKEYS
TRAITORS PROSTITUTES
MUD CORRUPT POLITICIANS
WORMS ETC...
UNRIGHTEOUS

THE GOAL IS TO BE HERE!

DON'T GET TOO EXCITED IF YOU'RE IN HERE.

BEING USED BY GOD ≠ BELONGING TO GOD

66 IF JESUS WAS SERIOUS . . . THEN BEING USED BY GOD IS NOT THE SAME AS BELONGING TO GOD.

NEAR THE END of the Sermon on the Mount, Jesus says that many will come to Him at the final judgment and appeal to their powerful works as evidence of their righteousness. Yet Jesus will say to them, "I never knew you." This scene raises a perplexing question for many of us: If these false Christians did not know Jesus or possess His Spirit, how were they able to perform miracles and drive out demons in His name? There is a story from the Old Testament that may help us answer this dilemma.

When God's people were in the wilderness without food or water they complained to Moses. Turning to the Lord for a solution, Moses was commanded to speak to a rock and water would flow from it for the people to drink. But Moses disobeyed God's command. Rather than speaking to the rock, he struck it twice with his staff. The Lord punished Moses severely for his irreverence and disobedience by forbidding him from entering the promised land.

The story appears straightforward, except for what happened when Moses disobeyed: the water flowed from the rock abundantly. A miracle still occurred. From a human point of view, Moses's ministry was effective, full of power, and praiseworthy. From God's point of view, however, Moses failed and his ministry at the waters of Meribah was rejected.

Could the same thing be happening to the false Christians Jesus describes in Matthew 7? Is it possible that because of His grace and care for His people, God chooses to sometimes display His power through ungodly leaders; to work in spite of them rather than because of them? We must not confuse being used by God with belonging to God.

 READ MORE **Numbers 20:10–13; John 6:28–35**

THE PROMISE (& LIE) OF MISSIONALISM

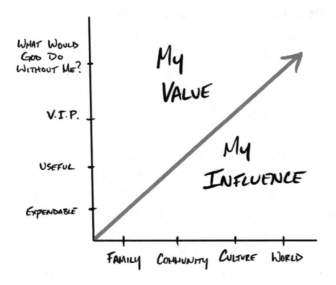

My
VALUE

My
INFLUENCE

WHAT WOULD
GOD DO
WITHOUT ME?

V.I.P.

USEFUL

EXPENDABLE

FAMILY   COMMUNITY   CULTURE   WORLD

67 IF JESUS WAS SERIOUS . . . THEN DEVOTION TO GOD'S MISSION IS NOT THE SAME AS DEVOTION TO GOD.

WE LIVE IN AN age of activism. We celebrate people who "change the world," and we believe our value is linked to the magnitude of our influence. This same spirit is evident in Christian communities, although it is often framed in the language of "mission."

The mission may be defined differently across various

church traditions. Some focus on the proclamation of the gospel and evangelism. Others emphasize the social reform of unjust systems. More charismatic traditions magnify the importance of spiritual battle against evil forces. No matter how the mission is defined, we tend to determine the authenticity of a person's faith, as well as their value, by how devoted they are to the works of God.

That is why we ought to soberly consider the warning of Jesus in Matthew 7:21–23. There He rejects people who committed their lives to preaching God's truth, spiritual warfare, and mighty works of transformation. They had falsely concluded that being used by God was evidence that they belonged to God. They had forgotten that God can, and often does, use ungodly characters to advance His work.

The assumption that activism for God is equivalent to acceptance by God is known as "missionalism." Gordon MacDonald defines it as "the belief that the worth of one's life is determined by the achievement of a grand objective."[1] This is a very real danger in many Christian communities. As the Sermon on the Mount reveals, it is entirely possible to spend one's life devoted to God's mission as a substitute for being devoted to God Himself.

 READ MORE **Revelation 2:1–5; Philippians 3:7–11**

PART 9

BE
SMART

"Everyone then who hears these words of mine and does them will be like a wise man who built his house on the rock. And the rain fell, and the floods came, and the winds blew and beat on that house, but it did not fall, because it had been founded on the rock. And everyone who hears these words of mine and does not do them will be like a foolish man who built his house on the sand. And the rain fell, and the floods came, and the winds blew and beat against that house, and it fell, and great was the fall of it."

And when Jesus finished these sayings, the crowds were astonished at his teaching, for he was teaching them as one who had authority, and not as their scribes.

MATTHEW 7:24-26

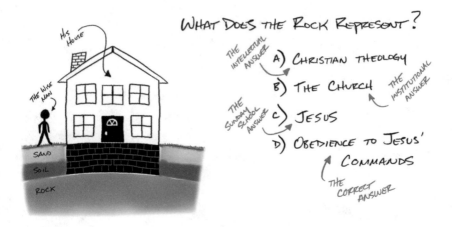

WHAT DOES THE ROCK REPRESENT?

THE INTELLECTUAL ANSWER → A) CHRISTIAN THEOLOGY

B) THE CHURCH ← THE INSTITUTIONAL ANSWER

THE SUNDAY SCHOOL ANSWER → C) JESUS

D) OBEDIENCE TO JESUS' COMMANDS ← THE CORRECT ANSWER

HIS HOUSE

THE WISE MAN

SAND
SOIL
ROCK

68

IF JESUS WAS SERIOUS . . . THEN A WISE PERSON MAY NOT BE EASY TO IDENTIFY.

JESUS ENDS HIS sermon with one of the best-known parables in the Bible. He contrasts a wise man who built his house on rock with a foolish man who built his house on sand. It is a simple image easily understood—even by children. In essence, what Jesus is saying is, "Don't be stupid." Perhaps the simplicity of the story explains why it's so frequently found in Sunday school songs and Bible curricula for kids.

The simplicity of the story, and its don't-be-stupid

message, make its common misinterpretation ironic. In my experience, those who are most familiar with the story are also the most likely to misread Jesus' intent. As a child, I was told that the man who built his house on the rock was a metaphor for Christians, and that the foolish man represented non-Christians. A plain reading of the story, however, reveals something much different.

The parable is about two houses that appear to be the same, the only difference exists below the surface. Jesus is not comparing Christians and non-Christians; he is contrasting two kinds of Christians—the genuine and the false. The wise person and the foolish one, according to Jesus, look the same. As John Stott said, "Both read the Bible, go to church, listen to sermons and buy Christian literature. The reason you often cannot tell the difference between them is that the deep foundations of their lives are hidden from view."[1]

The parable reminds us that the most important thing about us—what defines our life and destiny—is hidden from the view of others. It cannot be seen or praised by those around us. Therefore, if we live for the affirmation of others, we are unlikely to give much attention to our foundations, and we will be in great peril. Jesus says it is the secret, hidden reality upon which we construct our identity that matters most. The world celebrates the grandeur of the house, but the Lord alone knows the quality of its foundation.

 READ MORE **Matthew 6:2–6; Galatians 1:10**

WHAT IS UNSEEN DEFINES EVERYTHING

VISIBLE

INVISIBLE

UNSEEN
PATTERNS OF
OBEDIENCE

69 IF JESUS WAS SERIOUS . . .
THEN OUR UNSEEN DISCIPLINES ARE
WHAT MAKE OUR FAITH STRONG.

I WILL CONFESS that I enjoyed watching *Downton Abbey*, the snooty British television drama. The show followed the visible and invisible lives of an aristocratic English manor in the early twentieth century. Downton's upstairs inhabitants lived in a serene environment of luxury, stiff collars, and afternoon tea. Like an elegant swan, however, all the frantic work happened below the surface. Downstairs was filled with the constant commotion of servants, cooks, butlers, footmen, and chambermaids.

174

Without their endless work, the upstairs' illusion of ease would not be possible.

Downton Abbey is not unlike Jesus' parable about houses and foundations at the end of the Sermon on the Mount. He emphasizes that it is the unseen, buried part of the house that determines its ability to endure, not the glamorous qualities above the surface.

Recent studies say that increasing numbers of Christians, particularly young adults, are falling away from the faith. I wonder whether part of the problem is a form of pop Christianity that's more focused on building impressive houses rather than strong foundations. Life upstairs is easy and often fun. This is the life of exciting church events and activities. Life downstairs is much more difficult. This is the life of prayer, solitude, confession, and discipline; it's where the house is truly maintained.

To persevere in the Christian life, we must be willing to spend time in the servants' quarters and cellars to establish unseen—and uncelebrated—patterns of obedience.

 READ MORE **Jeremiah 17:7–8; Ephesians 3:14–19**

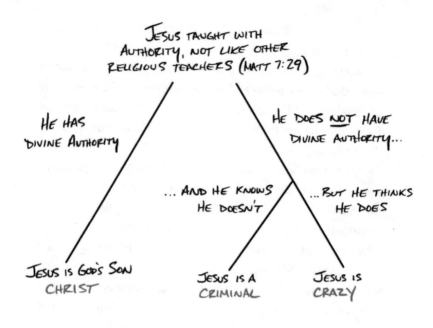

JESUS TAUGHT WITH AUTHORITY, NOT LIKE OTHER RELIGIOUS TEACHERS (MATT 7:29)

HE HAS DIVINE AUTHORITY

HE DOES **NOT** HAVE DIVINE AUTHORITY...

... AND HE KNOWS HE DOESN'T

...BUT HE THINKS HE DOES

JESUS IS GOD'S SON CHRIST

JESUS IS A CRIMINAL

JESUS IS CRAZY

70 IF JESUS WAS SERIOUS . . . THEN EITHER HE WAS CRAZY OR HE IS THE CHRIST.

MATTHEW WRITES that after Jesus finished His sermon, the crowds were "astonished at his teaching, for he was teaching them as one who had authority, and not as their scribes." Most rabbis of that day gained credibility and a following by appealing to their educational resume. They publicized what schools they attended, what highly regarded religious scholar they studied under, and often cited well-known biblical experts in their sermons to give them more credibility.

Jesus did none of those things.

In other words, other scribes taught by authority while Jesus taught with authority. This explains why His audience was astonished. Jesus was declaring a profound understanding of God's law without referencing any other historical source or rabbinical scholar. He was speaking as if He was God Himself. To assume such authority in that culture meant Jesus was either suffering from a severe case of delusion, He was deliberately lying about His authority and willfully committing blasphemy, or He really did possess the authority of the Almighty; He was either crazy, a criminal, or the Christ.[1]

How do you read the teachings of Jesus? Have you thought of the Sermon on the Mount as a moral code worthy of consideration? Jesus' listeners would not have seen that as a possible interpretation. Like them, we must decide whether Jesus is evil, out of His mind, or is actually speaking the authoritative words of God.

 READ MORE **Luke 5:17–26; Mark 11:27–33**

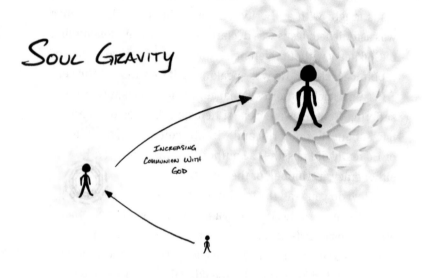

SOUL GRAVITY

INCREASING COMMUNION WITH GOD

71 **IF JESUS WAS SERIOUS . . . THEN WE SHOULD BE DRAWN TOWARD SUBSTANCE MORE THAN STYLE.**

GRAVITY'S ROLE IN our lives is so constant that we rarely think about it, but its force is one of the most powerful in the cosmos. Albert Einstein determined that the gravitational force of some celestial objects can even bend space and time.

I think there is a parallel between gravity's power and souls. Most of the people we encounter each day are rather ordinary. We don't think much about them. Some we like, others we don't. Occasionally, we encounter a soul with more mass, a person with a gravity that seems to bend the world around them. We are drawn to them for inexplicable reasons, and when they speak, our hearts burn within us. It isn't their appearance that draws us to them, nor do they necessarily possess greater knowledge or physical prowess. Instead, there is an authority to the person that defies common explanation.

I suspect this is what the crowds felt as Jesus preached. They were astonished by His words, confounded by His authority, and recognized that He was unlike other ordinary teachers. What Jesus' listeners felt, and what we feel around those with soul gravity, is the presence of the divine.

There are many earthly things that attract us to people, but what we long for and what we need most is God Himself. Mark Labberton described a season of visiting many different churches, searching for this kind of soul gravity: "Week by week, I was hungry for something. Hot, hip, techno worship was not what I wanted. Nor was it a particular kind of music, tradition, liturgy, or church size. I longed for some assurance and evidence of the gravity of God for ordinary life, for encouragement that the gospel was the defining and drawing Center from which all other dimensions of life could be lived."[1]

Are you aware of what is really drawing your soul? What are you attracted to? And are you eager to be drawn into the presence of God?

 READ MORE **Luke 24:28–35; Mark 6:1–6**

72 IF JESUS WAS SERIOUS . . . THEN HE IS THE SMARTEST PERSON EVER.

WHEN WE BEGAN this exploration of the Sermon on the Mount, we asked a simple but important question, "What if Jesus was serious?" Did He actually intend for us to do what He taught in His sermon? Are we to really love our enemies, not worry, and live without judgment? So many Christians today celebrate Jesus as "Lord" and "Savior," but then dismiss what He taught as impractical—or even impossible.

That was not a mistake that Jesus' original audience made. They marveled at His teaching and were particularly struck by the authority of His words. There was no mistaking the seriousness of His commands. Our problem, I think, is that pop Christianity has emphasized Jesus' love but ignored His intelligence. We treat Him like a benevolent old uncle who gives us advice because He truly cares for us, but deep down we suspect He doesn't understand how the modern world really works. So, we dismiss His well-meaning input.

Confronting this assumption, Dallas Willard wrote,

> Our commitment to Jesus can stand on no other foundation than a recognition that he is the one who knows the truth about our lives and our universe. It is not possible to trust Jesus, or anyone else, in matters where we do not believe him to be competent. We cannot pray for his

help and rely on his collaboration in dealing with real life matters we suspect might defeat his knowledge or abilities. And can we seriously imagine that Jesus could be Lord if he were not smart? If he were divine, would he be dumb? Or uninformed? Once you stop to think about it, how could he be what we take him to be in all other respects and not be the best-informed and most intelligent person of all, the smartest person who ever lived?[1]

Jesus is smart. Jesus is serious. Imagine how your life would be different if you took Him at His word. And imagine how our world would be different if those who claimed to follow Jesus actually did.

 READ MORE **Colossians 1:15–20; Revelation 1:12–18**

NOTES

INTRODUCTION

1. Tony Perkins, quoted in Edward-Isaac Dovere, "Tony Perkins: Trump Gets 'a Mulligan' on Life, Stormy Daniels" Politico, January 23, 2018, https://www.poliico.com/magazine/story/2018/01/23/tony-perkins-evangelicals-donald-trump-stormy-daniels-216498.
2. Michael Horton, "Beyond Culture Wars," *Modern Reformation*, May–June 1993, 3, quoted in Ronald J. Sider, "The Scandal of the Evangelical Conscience," *Books and Culture*, January/February 2005, https://www.booksandculture.com/articles/2005/janfeb/3.8.html.
3. George Barna, *Think Like Jesus: Make the Right Decision Every Time* (Nashville: Integrity, 2003), 40.

CHAPTER 1

1. Stanley Hauerwas, *Hannah's Child: A Theologian's Memoir* (Grand Rapids: Eerdmans, 2010), 38–39.

CHAPTER 2

1. Markham Heid, "You Asked: Is Social Media Making Me Miserable?," *Time*, August 2, 2017, https://time.com/4882372/social-media-facebook-instagram-unhappy/.
2. Scot McKnight, *The Story of God Bible Commentary: Sermon on the Mount* (Grand Rapids: Zondervan, 2013), 35.

CHAPTER 3

1. Dallas Willard, "The Gospel of the Kingdom," interview by Keith Giles, August 2005, http://old.dwillard.org/articles/artview.asp?artID=150.

CHAPTER 6

1. Theodore Parker, quoted in John Haynes Holmes et al., *Readings by Great Authors* (New York: Dodd, Mead and Company, 1918), 18, quoted by Martin Luther King Jr., https://quoteinvestigator.com/2012/11/15/arc-of-universe/.

CHAPTER 8

1. Caitlin Johnson, "Cutting Through Advertising Clutter," CBS, September 17, 2006, https://www.cbsnews.com/news/cutting-through-advertising-clutter/.

CHAPTER 10

1. John Stott, *The Message of the Sermon on the Mount* (Downers Grove, IL: Inter-Varsity Press, 1978), 52.

CHAPTER 13

1. John Stott, *The Message of the Sermon on the Mount* (Downers Grove, IL: Inter-Varsity Press, 1978), 67.

CHAPTER 19

1. Antonin Scalia, "Justice Scalia on the Record," interview by Lesley Stahl, *60 Minutes*, April 24, 2008, https://www.cbsnews.com/news/justice-scalia-on-the-record/.

CHAPTER 20

1. Dallas Willard, *The Divine Conspiracy* (San Francisco: HarperSanFrancisco, 1998), 151.
2. David Livingstone Smith, interview, "'Less Than Human': The Psychology of Cruelty," NPR.org, March 29, 2011, https://www.npr.org/2011/03/29/134956180/criminals-see-their-victims-as-less-than-human.

CHAPTER 23

1. Oswald Chambers, *Studies in the Sermon on the Mount* (Grand Rapids: Discovery House Publishers, 1960), 37.
2. Dallas Willard, *The Divine Conspiracy* (San Francisco: HarperSanFrancisco, 1998), 167.

CHAPTER 24

1. Fyodor Dostoevsky, *The Brothers Karamazov*, trans. Constance Garnett (New York: The Macmillan Company, 1922), 54.

CHAPTER 26

1. Ibid., 55.

CHAPTER 28

1. Dietrich Bonhoeffer, *Dietrich Bonhoeffer Works, Vol 5: Life Together and Prayerbook of the Bible* (Minneapolis: Fortress Press,1996), 90.

CHAPTER 29

1. Allyson Chiu, "More than 250 people worldwide have died taking selfies, study finds," *Washington Post*, October 3, 2018, https://www .washingtonpost.com/news/morning-mix/wp/2018/10/03/more-than-250-people-worldwide-have-died-taking-selfies-study-finds/.

CHAPTER 32

1. This quote is widely attributed to Oliver Wendell Holmes, but no original source has been located.

CHAPTER 34

1. Quoted in Timothy Garton Ash, "The Truth about Dictatorship," *The New York Review of Books*, February 19, 1998, 36–37.

CHAPTER 35

1. Ray Pritchard, "Does God Lead His Children Into Temptation?" KeepBelieving.com, October 10, 2009, https://www.keepbeliev ing.com/sermon/does-god-lead-his-children-into-temptation/.

CHAPTER 36

1. Dallas Willard, *The Divine Conspiracy* (San Francisco: HarperSan Francisco, 1998), 202.

CHAPTER 37

1. Martin Luther, *The Sermon on the Mount (Sermons) and the Magnificat*, Luther's Works, vol. 21, trans. and ed. Jaroslav Pelikan (St. Louis: Concordia, 1956), 155.

CHAPTER 41

1. From G. W. Offley, *A Narrative of the Life and Labors of Rev. G. W. Offley* (Hartford, CT: [s.n.], 1860), reprinted in *Five Black Lives* (Middletown, CT: Wesleyan University Press, 1971), 134–35; quoted in Albert J. Raboteau, *Slave Religion: The "Invisible Institution" in the Antebellum South* (New York: Oxford Press, 1978), 306.
2. Adapted from Skye Jethani, *With: Reimagining the Way You Relate to God* (Nashville: Thomas Nelson, 2011), 154–55.

CHAPTER 45

1. Henri Nouwen, *Spiritual Formation* (New York: HarperOne, 2010), 73.

CHAPTER 47

1. Quoted by Stan Friedman, "Greg Boyd: 'Judgmental Attitudes Keep Christians from Loving,'" Covenant Newswire, CovChurch.org, October 11, 2006, blogs.covchurch.org/newswire/2006/10/11/5189/.

CHAPTER 49

1. See Dallas Willard, *The Divine Conspiracy*, 231–32.

CHAPTER 51

1. Material in this chapter is adapted from Skye Jethani, "Stranded in Neverland," *Leadership Journal*, April 24, 2009. https://www.christianitytoday.com/pastors/2009/spring/strandedinneverland.html.

CHAPTER 52

1. C. S. Lewis, *God in the Dock*, ed. Walter Hooper (1970; Eerdmans, 2014), 107.

CHAPTER 53

1. Mohandas Gandhi, quoted in *The Wit and Wisdom of Gandhi*, ed. Homer A. Jack (1951; Mineola, NY: Dover Publications, 2005), 15.
2. Dallas Willard, *Knowing Christ Today* (New York: HarperOne, 2009), 89.

CHAPTER 54

1. See Jeremy Weber, "Christian, What Do You Believe? Probably a Heresy about Jesus, Says Survey," *Christianity Today*, October 16, 2018, https://www.christianitytoday.com/news/2018/october/what-do-christians-believe-ligonier-state-theology-heresy.html.

CHAPTER 56

1. Adapted from Skye Jethani, *The Divine Commodity: Discovering a Faith Beyond Consumer Christianity* (Grand Rapids: Zondervan, 2009), 159.

CHAPTER 57

1. Dietrich Bonhoeffer, *Discipleship* (Minneapolis: Fortress Press, 2015), 148–49.

CHAPTER 62

1. The quote is attributed to Mark Twain although the source is somewhat dubious. Still, the sentiment is valid.

CHAPTER 67

1. Gordon MacDonald, "Dangers of Missionalism," *Leadership Journal*, January 1, 2007, https://www.christianitytoday.com/pastors/2007/winter/16.38.html.

CHAPTER 68

1. John Stott with Douglas Connelly, *Reading the Sermon on the Mount with John Stott* (Downers Grove, IL: InterVarsity Press, 2016), 108.

CHAPTER 70

1. This is my spin on C. S. Lewis's brilliant "liar, lunatic, or Lord" argument found in his classic book, *Mere Christianity* (see the chapter "The Shocking Alternative"), to which many advocates of the faith are indebted.

CHAPTER 71

1. Mark Labberton, "Elemental Preaching," *Christianity Today*, January 17, 2010, https://www.christianitytoday.com/pastors/2010/winter/elementalpreaching.html.

CHAPTER 72

1. Dallas Willard, *The Great Omission: Reclaiming Jesus's Essential Teachings on Discipleship* (New York: HarperOne, 2006), 19.

WANT TO RECEIVE A DEVOTIONAL
EVERY MORNING FROM SKYE?

" LEAD US... "

TEMPTATION

GODS KINGDOM

EVIL

GOOD

RETHINKING SUCCESS IN MINISTRY

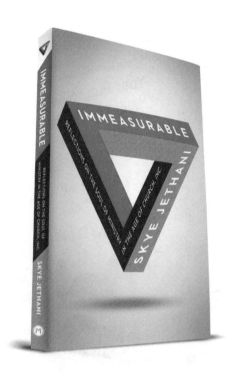

MOODY Publishers®

From the Word to Life®

Immeasurable helps ministers recognize the cultural forces shaping their view of the calling, and then reimagine what faithful church leaders can look like in the twenty-first century. Through short essays and reflections on the pastor's soul and skills, *Immeasurable* commends the true work of ministry—shepherding, teaching, encouraging—while redefining how we understand success in ministry.

978-0-8024-1619-3 | also available as eBook and audiobook

"Few books have the potential to change
your life as much as this one."
—Lee Strobel

**MOODY
Publishers**®

From the Word to Life®

Your Future Self Will Thank You is a compassionate and
humorous guide to reclaiming your willpower. It shares
proven, practical strategies for success, as well as biblical
principles that will help you whether you want to lose a few
pounds, conquer addiction, or kick your nail-biting habit.

978-0-8024-1829-6 | also available as eBook and audiobook